STRAP YOURSELF IN

STRAP YOURSELF IN

A MEMOIR OF MOTHERHOOD, DANCE FLOORS AND ALL THE MAYHEM IN BETWEEN

Amy Gerard

ALLEN&UNWIN
SYDNEY · MELBOURNE · AUCKLAND · LONDON

First published in 2024

Allen & Unwin
Cammeraygal Country
83 Alexander Street
Crows Nest NSW 2065
Australia
Phone: (61 2) 8425 0100
Email: info@allenandunwin.com
Web: www.allenandunwin.com

Allen & Unwin acknowledges the Traditional Owners of the Country on which we live and work. We pay our respects to all Aboriginal and Torres Strait Islander Elders, past and present.

 A catalogue record for this book is available from the National Library of Australia

ISBN 978 1 76147 014 1

Set in 12/19.5 pt Minion Pro by Midland Typesetters, Australia
Printed and bound in Australia by the Opus Group

10 9 8 7 6 5 4 3 2 1

To Charli, Bobby and Kobe
You are the unequivocal rays of light that
illuminate my journey in this world.

CONTENTS

INTRODUCTION

Hi guys!

It's Amy Gerard—better known as the sometimes dishevelled, sometimes glam mum of three kids who says out loud what most people only internalise. My hobbies include gyrating on the dance floor to 'Pony' and drinking rosé, but I'm so much more than that. I also love a good red, and margaritas on a hot day, and I can't go past a negroni on days that end in 'y'. I'm also really great at the Nutbush and if I haven't thrown my neck out after a night out on the town, you know I haven't really given it my all.

I love singing to old-school R&B music at the top of my lungs in a car, dancing around my living room with my dad to Cat Stevens, going on holidays (with and without my children), watching the sunset, trips to Mexico, and licking the salt and vinegar off each of my chips until I've murdered every tastebud on my tongue. Did I mention I love dancing?

I love making people happy and giving them my full attention when they want to be heard. I love walking at night-time when all the stars are out and there's no one else around. I love having fires down the back of my yard with my husband, smothering my kids with affection, a hot shower after a day at the beach, the smell of an exceptionally good bottle of red, and falling asleep knowing my kids are safe and sound a few metres away.

My dislikes include people who don't wave when you let them into traffic, open-mouth eaters, people who litter, open-mouth breathers, people who chew gum like bulldogs, two-faced people, slow walkers, people with no manners, slow eaters, slow talkers, poor oral hygiene, red onion and most white wines.

My most commonly used phrase in life is, 'Well, that didn't go as planned.' So this book is about the gaping chasm that exists between my expectations of life and the reality. Because the difference between the two can sometimes (read: all the time) be laughable.

From as early as primary school, we start to form expectations in our own heads of how our lives should be, and it's these kinds of expectations that can really fuck us over and leave us thinking, *Haaaaaaang on a second—this is not how I planned it in my head.* I don't know about you, but I had it *all* mapped out from the age of nine: the white picket fence that would wrap around our modest but also impeccably styled and always tidy house in the suburbs; my marriage at twenty-three to the love of my life, who would look almost identical to Devon Sawa and with whom I would always make love five times a week; the candlelit dinners we would share as I stared into his eyes. I would begin having children at the age of twenty-six and we would have four in total. The children would all take pride in their bedrooms, listen to what I had to say and eat all their dinner. I would also be an exceptional cook by this stage, with the patience of Mother Teresa. There would be no stress or mortgages, because at age nine I had only recently stopped eating my boogers and knew nothing of these things. I would go on to wear my permanently rose-coloured glasses for at least another eleven years.

I can't stress this enough: the expectations we put on ourselves as partners, friends, wives, mothers and humans in general are almost impossible to meet. Life is here to have fun with. The roller-coaster is actually the best part.

So you should know upfront that this is not going to be a self-help book, nor a life-coaching one. It won't teach you how to be better in bed or what to say when your three-year-old is flapping around like barramundi out of water in the middle of the cereal aisle at Woolies.

What I *hope* this book does for you is make you feel seen. Life can be a total shitshow but the best parts often happen unexpectedly. The best stories begin with, 'You'll never believe what happened', the best adventures were never perfectly planned, and the most important turning points in life will come, more often than not, at the most unexpected times.

I want this book to be a warm hug, or a metaphorical friend who you can laugh along with. I want it to take weight, guilt and shame off your shoulders. I want you to know that we are all individual humans with our own flaws and none of us get it right all the time, but most hardships come with growth and strength, and a resilience that sometimes lies dormant. (Holy shit, I've gone all Tony Robbins.)

Reality can be a real motherfucker, but if you can learn to roll with the punches and take your reality and make it your bitch, then your perspective will change. Before you know it, you'll be shitting out rainbows and hugging strangers while blades of sunshine beam out through your eyes.

Okay, the last bit was a stretch. But I do hope you'll find some joy or perspective or comfort in these pages.

Overall, my end goal is to be a really good human, laugh at the things I can't control and work on the things I can, leave people better than how I found them, ensure all dance floors are being utilised, make my parents proud and raise my kids right. In that order, too.

Love you all.

Mean it.

Amy x

THE EXPECTATION OF WRITING A BOOK

Writing a book is something that I have wanted to do for as long as I can remember. I don't profess to be an expert in anything, I won't be winning a Nobel Prize in Literature anytime soon, nor would I know how to write a steaming-hot romance novel, but I can tell you stories about the life I've lived till the cows come home.

If you ask my friends, they'll tell you that I'm the most laidback person in the world and yet somehow everything always works out for me. I believe that being chilled-out definitely helps in most situations, but I also had this thing growing up called 'Copp Luck' (Copp was my maiden name). My dad used to talk about it all the time. We would drive to the Royal Easter Show and get stuck in traffic, and Mum would say something like, 'We are never going to find a park', to which my dad would always reply, ''Course we will. We have Copp Luck on our side.' And he was right—without fail, at every mention of Copp Luck, we would sure as shit find a park, or a shop would open just as we were turning up, or the rain would stop just as I was about to step out onto the netball court.

As a kid, I believed everything my parents told me: that Santa and the Tooth Fairy were real, that crusts made your hair curly and that if I ate heaps of carrots I'd be able to see in the dark better, and I truly believed in the magic of being born into such a lucky family. Once, my brothers and I were playing hide-and-seek in the construction site of a half-built house in the neighbourhood. My little brother ran around a corner and off a ledge, accidentally landing on a pile of crushed bricks. I had been hiding in the portaloo at the time and could hear him crying. I ran out to find him covered head to toe in blood. I instantly scooped him into my arms and carried him home as fast as I could, but his forehead had been split open and was gushing blood. So I just kept repeating in my head: *He'll be okay. We've got Copp Luck. He'll be fine.* And he was. Was it mainly because my parents acted quickly and got him straight to the hospital for stitches? Probably. But it made me feel confident that, while good and bad things would happen during my life, we had luck on our side to help make sure things would work out okay.

I tried to switch the luck to my married name after taking my husband Rhian's surname, but 'Gerard Luck' doesn't really have the same ring to it.

I still subconsciously lean on this make-believe superpower all the time. It's why I don't worry too much about certain situations, like parking and applying for jobs, moving house and making my flight on time, because I always know things will work out. It infuriates my husband on the daily because he loves to get stressed out. I'm almost certain he thinks I'm some kind of stoned, wishy-washy sloth that moves at a snail's pace and stops to smell the flowers and talk to butterflies when there is shit going down, but I know we are going to get to the end goal eventually. (That sentence alone is going to piss him off when he reads it.) I just like to do things without the added stress, angst and sweaty upper lip.

I'm not sure that Copp Luck actually played a part in things working out, but it was the magic I needed growing up—an extra security blanket when life threw me curveballs—and it makes me feel like there are higher powers out there who always seem to have my back.

Now, at thirty-six, while acknowledging the wonderfully privileged life I had with my family, I know Copp Luck doesn't have anything to do with it. Really, it comes down to perspective. Our life hasn't always been smooth sailing. We lost our house in a bushfire in 1994 and were without a home for more than a year. Both my parents have battled cancer and there have been countless other health issues. There has been death and sadness and dark times too. But with every bit of shade there is always light, and Copp Luck has helped me remember that the way you look at your own fortunes and challenges can change everything.

So, as I prepare to impart my unsolicited words of wisdom (which absolutely nobody asked for) onto these pages, I know Copp Luck will play out somehow. I am sure there will be edits galore, swear words removed and chapters rewritten, but I also know we will get there eventually. My expectations of writing this book are that it will be fun, challenging, time-consuming, frustrating and incredibly rewarding, but you'll have to read the very last chapter to see if reality lived up to them.

PRESSURE IS ON, AMY.*

(*Me, talking to myself in the third person with a quivering butthole.)

CHILDHOOD

Expectation: Can't wait to give my kids the exact same one I had

Reality: Technology happened

I grew up as the eldest of three kids, and I took my role as self-proclaimed leader very seriously. Ben was twenty-two months younger than me and Tom was sixteen months behind him. I still like to tease them and call them my sisters (because I never got any real ones), and we all grew up wrestling, pushing each other down stairs, climbing trees, setting up obstacle courses and running each other up and down the street on discarded mattresses on wheels from council clean-ups. We built up each other's confidence with compliments. They would tell me it looked like I had been shat on through a flyscreen because I had freckles, we used to call Tom a sphere with no bones right before he went through puberty, and Ben was always Dad's favourite so naturally we called him an inbred. Real mature insults, you know. They never bothered any of us and I knew there was never any malice behind them. Our love language has always been softly bullying each other.

Even though they both tower over me now, I always felt like the big sister who needed to protect them. When I wasn't leading them

9

astray by showing them how to chew up a napkin and spit the tiny ball through a straw to land on our parents' faces at our favourite Chinese restaurant, or how to climb into wheelie bins and roll each other down the street, I was leading by example and teaching them the nice way to approach girls or what to wear on date nights.

We had a pretty idyllic childhood. We lived in a modest four-bedroom home in the suburb of Alfords Point, about forty-five minutes south of Sydney. It's classified as part of the Sutherland Shire but it is literally the ass end of it. When most people think of the Shire, they think of the coastal beaches of Cronulla but we are in fact about thirty minutes inland. Instead of the ocean, we back onto the bush and there are trees and trees as far as the eye can see if you walk into our backyard. Family holidays consisted of 2.5-hour drives down the south coast to where my nan lives in Vincentia, the occasional holiday over to Brighton in the UK to visit Mum's side of the family, and barbecues and picnics with friends who had become family. Summers were spent riding our bikes all day long, or running through sprinklers in the front or backyard. We would spend hours looking for four-leaf clovers or lying on our backs and making pictures out of the clouds. We were lucky that our house backed onto some major bushland, and the caves and secret hiding places were endless. We grew up with no fear. We didn't worry about spiders or snakes, both of which are very prominent in our backyard.

We would walk up to the nearby chicken shop and buy $1.50 worth of hot chips that would get dumped onto paper and wrapped up into a hot-chip burrito. Paddle Pops cost 80 cents each, and if Dad ever felt like splurging we would get Golden Gaytimes. We would take our own popcorn to the movies and always packed sandwiches for car rides. I wouldn't go as far as to say my dad's sphincter was tightly closed over for a lot of my childhood, but he definitely didn't like to spend money if he didn't have to. His favourite saying is, 'Look after the pennies and the pounds will look after themselves', and he drummed (read: lectured) this into me from a very young age. My dad's favourite topic of conversation is superannuation and how important it is. If anyone wants their ear chewed off about it, I can send him round. You had better be personally contributing to it or he will be disappointed.

We never had any junk food in the house, except maybe a packet of Milk Arrowroots, and if Dad ever wanted to get all extravagant he would go all out and buy Mint Slices, hide them in the fridge and ration them out to us like we were the luckiest kids in the world. The idea of having McDonald's at any point throughout the year felt like a dream. I'm almost certain that we only had it about four times in the space of a decade. Dad would always choose a banana squashed into the guts of a bread roll over 'that junk'. I didn't realise it at the time because I knew no different, but my parents were very strict. I make jokes about the von Trapp children, and we weren't far off.

We would eat dinner every night at 6.30 p.m. so we were finished in time for Dad to watch the 7 p.m. news on the ABC. It's still the only channel he ever watches. He would go around the table, asking each of us how our day was and what we got up to, and we would take it in turns to answer. Elbows were not allowed on the table, and if you didn't eat your dinner you went to bed hungry. We weren't allowed to watch *The Simpsons* and swearing was absolutely forbidden in the house. 'Hate' was too strong a word and if we said anything derogatory beginning with the letters S or F we would have hot English mustard applied to our tongues. Ironic to think that I *love* the stuff now.

But although my childhood was somewhat sheltered, and we lived on carrot sticks and apples and only got to watch the ABC for most of it, the thing I remember most was feeling safe. Always cared for, always loved. We didn't have the best of anything but we had each other and that was all that ever mattered. We always had each other. And I never had any reason to believe that would change.

In 1994, when I was eight, there were terrible bushfires around Sydney. So many houses were lost and ours was one of them. I remember the day like it was yesterday. We were having a barbecue in our backyard with a bunch of other families. It was a hot day but there was a bit of a breeze. We noticed a big, billowing smoke cloud suddenly appear from behind a huge gum tree. We jumped out of the pool to see where it was coming from and Mum assured me that it was miles away and that there was a river between us and the smoke. Slowly but surely, flames started getting a little bit higher and more visible to us on the other side of the gully. Mum suggested I go inside and pack a few things, just to be safe. She mentioned grabbing my nan's jewellery and anything else that held sentimental value to me. Naturally, because I had been deprived of junk food my whole life, I boycotted Nan's jewels and headed straight into the kitchen instead, where our family friends had brought over marshmallows and bags of Doritos—and these are the 'valuables' I ended up packing. You've got to laugh, right?

Mum and Dad suggested that us kids leave with one of our family friends, so we wrapped our towels around ourselves and jumped in the car. I was still a bit perplexed as to why we had been rushed out of the house, because after all there was a river between us and the flames, and fire couldn't cross water.

But that's exactly what it did—in the form of a fireball. While I was being driven to a nearby suburb in the safety of our family friends' car, Mum and Dad were watching on in panic as the flames landed in our backyard. Mum tells the story of Dad managing to whip out his camera and snap photos of the flames licking the sides of our wooden fences right before they engulfed the pickets. He snapped as many photos as he could before realising that he didn't even have film in the camera, while Mum managed to grab their wedding album. They jumped in my dad's car and reversed out of the driveway as the flames entered our family home. They managed to get out just as the suburb was completely shut down.

My brothers and I waited anxiously for Mum and Dad to arrive at our friends' place, and when they walked through the door, I knew the news wasn't good. Seeing the tears streaming down Mum's face, I started to feel a little bit scared and nervous. I don't think Mum and Dad really knew the extent of the damage at that point either, only that it had been looking pretty dire as they fled the street. My dad does this funny thing when he is emotional. He puffs out his chest and lowers his voice. He looks you directly in the eyes, and when he talks he sounds firm and direct and filled with conviction. That day, he puffed out his chest and told us that everything was going to be alright, and I believed him.

Mum and Dad left early the next morning to assess the damage to the house. They were only letting residents who lived in the suburb back in, so we got stuck waiting with our family friends until they came back. We couldn't drive into the street because it was sectioned off, but we could walk in because we lived there. As we got closer to where our house should have been, I realised I couldn't even see it. The two-storey, double-brick house that I had called home for the last eight years was merely a heap of blackened broken bricks. The smell was intense, and the grass and plants on either side of the house were gone. The house to the left of ours was still standing, and the house to the right had some damage to part of its roof but was mostly still intact. In the middle was a gap where my home used to be. Everything inside it had disintegrated under the heat of the flames. There were no longer stairs or doorways. Mum's car was sitting in the garage, a burned-out shell. Everything was black and there was still smoke coming off the entire block of land. The backyard was flattened, the pool fence had melted, and I could see the tiny remnants of a boogie board that had been left floating in the pool.

I kept looking to Mum and Dad—they were holding on tight to our hands and kept hugging us with tears welled up in their eyes. I knew they were struggling to keep it together. They were trying desperately to be brave for us. Dad kept reminding us: as long as we had each other, we would always be okay. I felt sad that I had lost all my favourite things in my bedroom and all the memories that I had created there. I felt sad that I didn't have somewhere to come home to, and all of a sudden the future felt so uncertain. I was scared but, just as Mum and Dad were being brave for us, I also felt that I had to be brave for my brothers. I was the big sister, after all.

Over the following days, we were allowed to walk into the house. The saddest part for me was finding things that had miraculously survived the fire. Little trinkets that used to disappear among our other belongings were now the only things we had left. Mum managed to find a little jewellery box (made of paper, of all things) that had somehow survived, and we collected coins and toy cars from the boys' room.

With Mum's family living in England and Dad's closest family member being two-and-a-half hours away, we relied heavily on the love and support of friends and the community. In the darkest of situations, I can't tell you the magical way people rally around you. Total strangers would drive out of their way to drop clothes off to us. We were given school uniforms from friends, and our backpacks were replaced. The Red Cross was incredible, as were all of my dad's old police prosecutor mates. I remember them coming to visit us when we were staying at a friend's place—they had dressed up like Santa Claus (in the middle of January) to deliver us presents. We had lost all the Christmas presents that had arrived with Santa the month earlier. We got rollerblades and new bikes and other things that brought huge grins to our faces. There was a photo taken by someone with us kids looking like we had won the lotto and my mum standing in the doorway behind us with her hands up to her face, overcome with emotion. It wasn't until recently that I began to understand the magnitude of what her emotions must have been like that day. While the next twelve months looked incredibly different for us, sleeping on beds or couches or in caravans at different friends' places, my dad's words rang true: as long as we had each other, we would always be okay.

I was offered counselling through the school but I truly didn't feel like I needed it. We rebuilt our house on the same block of land, which I thought was ridiculous at the time, but life slowly and surely moved on.

But the things you go through as a young child have funny ways of popping up again in your adult life. Some things manifest into trauma, some change the path you're on and some lay dormant in your brain until something triggers the memory. It's only recently that I have dealt with some pretty heavy feelings about those 1994 bushfires—not because I lost my home, but because every time I smell bushfire smoke I look back on that year from a different perspective. All I can think about these days is how hard it would have been for my mum and dad.

I now know that the minute your children come into the world, a lot of things change, but protecting them and keeping them safe is your absolute number-one priority. I think of how terrifying it must have been for Mum to not know where she would be putting us to bed at night. I know all too well that as a parent you need to maintain a level of calm in situations that could otherwise truly traumatise your kids. And that's exactly what they did. They stayed level-headed as their home burned to the ground. They stayed strong and brave for us in the aftermath and made sure we felt nothing but safe and secure, no matter where we were.

We moved through life side by side. Teenage Amy was a bit of a dick to her parents, I must admit. Dad and I clashed quite a lot, because he always wanted to protect me and I always wanted to go out. I pushed the boundaries a *lot*, which paved the way for my brothers to look like absolute angels in comparison. You're welcome, Ben and Tom. Mum consistently played the calm role and Dad was the big silverback gorilla who was fiery and sometimes struggled to regulate his emotions, especially when we were younger.

That said, one of the things I have always admired most about my dad is his ability to repair situations. There's a guilt we parents feel when we lose our cool—and I'm not talking about refusing to play with your kids while you are trying to cook dinner or refusing to read them one extra book at bedtime. I mean the *real* losing-our-cool guilt, which is indicative of our own morality: it's a sign that we can acknowledge our mistakes and our sometimes poor decisions. As humans we aren't perfect, nor are we designed to experience one emotion throughout life. We have our ups and downs, our good days and our bad days, and I've never felt like there was anything wrong with showcasing a full spectrum of feelings. When Dad and I would butt heads in my teenage years, I would usually storm off or end up raging in my bedroom. Every single time, he'd come and talk me through his feelings and explain why things had escalated.

He has always taught me to repair my arguments—not just with him, but with Mum and my brothers and my partners. We would talk things through and release the bad feelings through forgiveness and love. It's something that I have seen him do for my entire life, and I've carried it into my own parenting skill set.

My parents have been an unwavering constant in my life. Even when they are travelling, they are there. Even now that we have grown up and left the nest, they still play a huge role in my life.

Now it's my turn to make sure I give my own children the same kind of magical upbringing.

So how am I doing so far, I hear you ask?

Well, listen, we might be almost three decades along since eight-year-old Amy smuggled Doritos out of her house shortly before it burned to the ground, and while so much in the world has changed, present-day Amy is trying her absolute hardest to recreate her own youth for her children. But there's this thing called the internet and while it was around when I was a kid, we never really paid it much attention: you had to dial up a modem and then wait for it to connect, and then the house phone would ring and your internet connection would get cut off immediately. Fast-forward to 2023 and the internet is more easily accessible than pingers at a festival.

So while six-year-old me was singing into a freestanding floor fan to make my voice go funny, my kids can watch live videos of pretty much anything they want. Seven-year-olds now look like they're eighteen and young girls seem to be skipping over that awkward pre-puberty stage where everyone looked a little bit like Warwick Capper and Fatty Vautin (or was that just me?).

You want to watch a video of slime being made? It's there for you. A peacock grooming its own legs? No worries. Two grandparents from Germany raising a bear in their house? Here, have a series. The list of what you can find on the internet is literally endless and here's where I have a problem.

I don't want my kids to be glued to iPads and mobile phones. My brothers and I were running home from school to see who could get into their swimmers and jump into the pool the quickest, but mine will run through the door and have a meltdown because their iPad hasn't charged. I'm in a constant battle with myself (and more so with my children) because I am so desperately trying to hold onto the childhood I knew and loved and want for my own kids, but times have changed and life is constantly evolving. And it feels like if we don't jump on the moving train, we will all get left behind.

Trying to force my thirty-year-old childhood memories onto my kids, who have been born into a very different era, is like pushing shit uphill sometimes. For years I wouldn't let any of my kids have an iPad. I was adamant that they didn't need one. But when my eldest child, Charli, finally started school I felt like my hands were tied. There were tablets in the classroom. There was no escaping them and yet I still refused to have one at home.

Was I being unfair? Was I fighting the inevitable? The jury is still out on both. If you had asked Charli, I was ruining her life. But I somehow still felt like I was doing the right thing by her, whether she chose to see it or not.

I'm conscious that for parents, iPads, tablets, laptops, Nintendos, smartphones and TVs—all the screens—often make our days easier.

Life is busy, and the peaceful and quiet downtime that accompanies a kid being glued to an iPad or phone is quite frankly endlessly appealing. But I feel such a strong urge to push back and force them out into the backyard. Build caves. Climb into wheelie bins. Look at the clouds. Use your imagination. Make mud pies. *Get dirty.* Why are kids so grossed-out by everything these days?

In fairness, it's not entirely their fault. As the world has changed, so too has our knowledge about the dangers that exist. My trampoline never had a net around it. My car seat didn't have a four-point harness. My kids aren't even allowed to run on the asphalt at school without getting in trouble. Kids absorb everything, and maybe they've absorbed some of our generation's cautiousness. There is no way my daughter would climb down into the bush and go on an adventure to find caves. Children are cautious of everything: spiders, lizards, creepy crawlies. All the things that used to fascinate me as a kid. The world has levelled up to protect kids as much as possible, which in many ways is wonderful, but sometimes I wonder what kind of childhood I would have preferred for my kids. I'm constantly torn between acknowledging the amazing opportunities they have today and wondering if a simpler life wasn't so bad after all. Bullying wasn't able to follow you home from school, and if your friend said she was going to call you on the home phone at 4.15 p.m., you'd sit by it and wait. We learned how to be patient, and how to make our own fun, because we were expected to and there were no other options. In this world of instant gratification and blurred social boundaries, it's harder to teach our kids the same lessons.

When I became a parent, I set out with all the best intentions. I took the best bits from my own upbringing and tried to apply them to a completely different world. Have I lived up to my own self-made precedent? Absolutely not. Do I sometimes think that I should just lean into the reality that is our technology-focused future? Sure. Will I be doing everything in my power to make sure that until then my kids are spending as much time as possible outdoors? You bet I will.

I used to make up stories at night to share with my kids, talking about them in the third person and adding in all the things I remembered about growing up. Most of the words they wouldn't have even understood, but I was convinced I could write a children's book one day about the parallels and differences we had growing up.

The stories always went a little something like this:

Once upon a time, in a land not so far away, there existed a generation of kids who roamed the earth with an abundance of imagination and a shortage of gadgets. But oh, how times have changed. Fast-forward thirty years and you'll find yourself in a world of childhood where technology reigns supreme and kids have a whole new set of hilarious adventures.

Charli, Bobby and Kobe are adventure protagonists. They are wild whirlwinds of curiosity armed with iPads that seem to be permanently attached to their hands. (YES, I'M LOOKING AT YOU THREE!) Gone are the days of walkie-talkies and bicycles being the primary means of communication and transport. Nowadays, kids have their own social media profiles, and they use Messenger Kids to speak to their friends through emojis or videos that have graphics turning them into rainbow unicorns while they talk.

Back in my day, if you wanted a recipe, you'd have to open a cookbook and follow the instructions. But in today's world everything is just a voice command away and you can even watch tutorial videos on how to make something from the comfort of your own kitchen.

Bobby walks downstairs to find his dad going through old photo albums. He finds himself captivated by the pictures of his dad and older brother jumping on the trampoline, with not a safety net in sight. There's photos of him and his friends deep inside caves making mud cakes. He can't believe that there were no virtual-reality headsets or holographic video games back then. Where are the pics of him playing Roblox?

His dad explains that back in his childhood they had to use their own imaginations to have fun. They built forts out of blankets, played Red Light Green Light with their friends and got creative with the simplest of toys. It was a different kind of adventure.

Charli, Bobby and Kobe really love the sound of that. Maybe, every now and again, they could also leave their iPads inside for a minute and step outside into the beautiful sunshine, and really lean into the adventures that Mum and Dad speak of so fondly.

More often than not, Bobby leaves before my story has finished to jump back on to his Roblox game and Charli interrupts to ask me whether or not I've paid for her dance concert via the app. Oh, and I need to upload some photos of her in her costume to make sure the sizing is correct. Kobe, bless his little soul, is still being deprived of an iPad because he's only four, but spent the last six months leaning over Bobby's shoulder and being equally drawn in (read: addicted) to the screen, watching Ninja Kidz. He now runs at me with karate moves every time I say no to another biscuit.

Life is so very different and maybe I'm holding onto a period in history that simply doesn't look the same in today's world, but when I put them to bed at night and watch them fall asleep, they don't look so different to how I looked at the same age. The reality is that while we live in an era of ubiquitous iPads and screens, my kids' childhood is still brimming with love. The reason I bought the house that we live in today is because it reminds me of everything I had and everything I want for my kids, and in a perfect world they might just be able to have a little bit of both. They will still grow up in a family that supports them, lifts them up and protects them at all costs. Rhian and I will forever remain their safe space, and we will go on holidays and adventures down the coast to create our own memories as often as we can.

Above all, I want their childhood to be a tapestry of love, laughter and unforgettable experiences. Something that will lay the foundation for a happy and fulfilling life, the same way mine did for me. Their childhood might not look identical to mine, but hopefully I'm doing enough (screen-time management) so this special time in their lives is carried in their hearts forever.

RELATIONSHIPS

Expectation: Meet boy, develop feelings, become boyfriend and girlfriend, kiss, marry, die

Reality: As my wise nan always said, 'You've gotta kiss a whole lot of frogs before you meet your prince'

The way Mum and Dad interacted when I was young set the benchmark for how I imagined a romantic relationship should look. They would hold hands everywhere they went, and slow dance with each other in the lounge room. They were the best teammates, playing to their strengths, one always stepping in with what the other lacked, and from the outside looking in I truly thought their relationship was perfect. So I wasn't going to settle for anything less.

Naturally, my expectations grew from there, and of course they became more unrealistic and far-fetched as the years went on. They varied from roses being left on my door weekly to being showered with words of affirmation daily. My fantasy partner and I would both be equally committed to the relationship, and mutual trust in one another would be a given. There would be a shared affection and appreciation of each other, and empathy for the experiences and emotions we didn't understand. I had an intense love affair in my head with Devon Sawa after seeing the movie *Casper the Friendly Ghost* at about age thirteen, and I would daydream about him more than I care to admit. He was the perfect boyfriend I never even went out with, but I just knew we would have been amazing together.

I carried loads of unrealistic expectations into my very first relationship. I just *knew* that this feeling would never die. We'd never get bored of each other or even look in the direction of anyone else. Lust would live on for eternity, as would patience and an understanding of my monthly bleed (read: hormonally imbalanced rage). There would be understanding about my much-needed girl time, compromises *always*, and a profound respect for and interest in each other's differences. There would be no yelling or nasty words thrown each other's way and our relationship would be built upon a friendship that would stand the test of time. He would love accompanying me to get my nails done. I would never let him watch the footy without me, and I would cheer on whatever team it was he went for. Those butterflies that you get at the beginning of every relationship stick around forever, right?

But relationships are never, ever that simple, and no one can keep their rose-coloured glasses on for long. Just like every roller-coaster I've ever been on, my dating history has had its ups and downs. I've wanted to eject myself from some moving roller-coasters, or get off as soon as I've sat down, and there was one that I wanted to ride for way longer—even though the ride had well and truly come to an end.

I can count on one hand the girlfriends who met a partner at school, planted a kiss on their face and stayed with them happily— to this day. I take my hat off to them, really, because it must be nice living in a blissful world of knowing nothing else. Nor do they care to see what someone else's grass looks like or what a relationship with someone else might consist of.

I'm not sure if it's because I have a short attention span or because I *absolutely* love the first six months of any relationship, but I have been through my fair share of relationships. I chase that intense oxytocin hit that comes with meeting someone for the first time and getting those warm and fuzzies (and not just in your tummy!). Being in love makes me feel giddy and high, like someone has ignited a firework of feelings in my gut and/or dropped some MDMA into my drink and life is good. I love the feeling, and I really enjoy sharing my life with a partner. So it's no surprise that I bounced around a few (read: a lot of) relationships.

When I was younger I was convinced that *every* guy I dated was The One. I was fifteen when I got asked out for the first time and entered into my first boyfriend/girlfriend relationship. Even though I was still learning how to insert a tampon properly, I would spend every waking minute with my boyfriend. I made him wait nine months before we took our relationship to the 'home run' status. I remember being terrified, thinking it was going to hurt, but nine months of foreplay—where nothing actually really happened, but we would gyrate our naked bodies on top of each other, pretending— was enough to get me ready. Welcome to my first sexual experience. It was wonderful and the beginning of me becoming a supercharged Energizer sex bunny. I felt safe and I was completely comfortable with him, and being intimate with the love of my life made total sense. After all, this was the guy I was going to marry. Playing it cool was for losers and when I wasn't writing my boyfriend love letters, I was writing his initials on everything I owned. I went over to the UK for a family holiday, and in eighteen days I somehow managed to write him a sixty-four-page book. There is no chill when it comes to young love and I let it consume me.

And then, eighteen months after starting, it ended, and I felt a pain I had never experienced in my life. Your first heartbreak is like nothing you can prepare yourself for. Even if you're the one who did the breaking up because you realised that there was so much of the world you wanted to see and you couldn't possibly only have ridden *one* penis . . . *cough* I mean, kissed *one* frog . . .

You spiral with confusion about whether you've made the right decision. You desperately want to go and travel the world and live outside of your suburb and meet new people but *what about the three kids we were meant to have, with the white picket fence?* Then he hates you and you have so much regret. It feels as if life can't go on, as if there's no way you will recover from your heart being pulled out of your chest through an open cavity. I was only seventeen, but if you think about the pain of a broken relationship at such a pivotal moment in life, you'll know how dramatic and jarring the feeling is. It was like my soul was being crushed. If only I could go back in time and give myself a little pep talk, like, *Pull yourself together, babes. You've got at least another ten relationships ahead of you!* There was no crying over a tub of ice cream in bed. I couldn't eat. I couldn't sleep, either, and every morning for a brief second I felt like it could all be one very bad nightmare . . . until I opened my eyes and realised that *this* was my new reality.

Your first relationship is the one that has an everlasting impact. It's bittersweet. I moved through the next five years thinking of him often. What's that saying? *You never forget your first.*

Fast-forward a decade when, as a seasoned 'relationship' gal, I realised that not a single boyfriend had *ever* lived up to all of the expectations I listed earlier in this chapter. Not only that, but even as a teenager I realised that it was going to be hard for me to find a relationship that mirrored my parents', because in order to do that I would have to be more like my mum ... and I am, in fact, a hundred per cent my dad.

My parents have quite the old-school relationship. My mum is English and her parents were even more old-school. You know how in the olden days the men would go out to work and the women would stay home and have kids (which, of course, still happens— look at me)? And the man was a more dominant head of the house, while the woman took on a more submissive role? I grew up watching this kind of dynamic as a kid, and while I dreamed of having a love as calm and secure as Mum and Dad's, I also thought to myself, *I never want to be in a relationship where I feel like my opinion will always be overruled by a male.* That balance didn't feel right to me, although in my parents' eyes both parties were playing to their strengths and life was harmonious.

When I was growing up, Mum always cooked dinner, and we would all sit around the table as a family to eat. Once we were finished, Dad would ask me to clear the plates and wash up, and I couldn't wrap my head around the fact that I had to do this while my brothers just got to sit at the table. *Why the hell am I washing up while the boys do nothing? What is this, the sixties?* I was livid at the injustice.

But while I perceived my parents' marriage to be a dated one, it absolutely worked for them because they both enjoyed the roles they played within it. My dad has always been the breadwinner, the provider, the man of the house; Mum was the nurturer, who raised us and was always present and did everything else around the house. I distinctly remember sitting at the top of the stairs one night, listening to my parents having an argument downstairs. They very rarely argued and never in front of us when they did, but I had been lying awake in bed and overheard a commotion. It was over something ridiculous like the house being messy but my dad was shouting and yelling and my mum just spoke calmly and then eventually was silent. I sat there on the stairs clenching my fists, wanting so desperately to go down and stick up for Mum. It infuriated me that she wasn't standing up for herself, that she was allowing Dad to blame her and raise his voice, even if it was over something so trivial. When I spoke to her about it the next day, she told me there was no point in yelling back. She would just silently nod and let him go on his yelling rant, and then eventually he would calm down and apologise to her. As a teenager sitting on the stairs listening, I viewed her position in the argument as weak, but she was actually the wiser, more mature one out of the two of them. It's how she has handled everything in her life and I wish more than anything that I was more like her.

For quite some time in my early dating years I couldn't under-stand why all the relationships I was getting myself into were so challenging. And then it dawned on me: I was the yeller. I was basically 'the man' in all of them, and I took on the dominant role. The older I got, the more I realised that I wouldn't be able to play the same role as Mum. I'm a lovely person (if I do say so myself) but if you push my buttons, I'm far too lippy and hot-headed—I have my dad's blood running through my veins. We are emotional beings who wear our hearts on our sleeves. I knew I didn't want to be Miss Trunchbull with only timid Labrador puppies as partners, though, so my quest for an equal began.

I dated everyone from my high school sweetheart to the obsessive-compulsive, controlling guy. There was the older man, the Pom, the younger man, the puppy dog, the so-sweet-I-could-barely-handle-breaking-up-with-him one, the bad boy(s), the one cheating on his wife (I can safely say I didn't know about her—until she tried to run me over with her car) and the downright batshit-crazy one. I don't think I was without a boyfriend for a good twelve years of my life. Not because I was dependent on a partner to make myself feel better, but because I genuinely *love* sharing my life with someone else. Dating so many different kinds of guys might sound like an absurd way to go about it, but not only was it a bloody good time, it truly helped me to work out which things were non-negotiable and which things I could totally live without. I took something away from every single guy I dated. It was like creating a mental checklist of wants, and after a decade of dating I could almost write a recipe for the exact guy I knew I wanted to settle down with.

My high school sweetheart taught me that being with someone who was family oriented was an absolute must, given I was so close to mine. He lived down the street from me, and my family became his and vice versa. He was just as close to his own family, and they were always a huge priority in his life. Having such similar upbringings meant that spending so much time with each other's families felt completely normal. We spent almost every day together either at his house or mine, and went away on holidays together. He could almost have passed for another family member except for the fact we were bumping privates when no one was looking. I loved how easy and natural that felt and how warmly his family had accepted me. 'Family oriented' was definitely in my top three wants. So I added it to the recipe.

The next guy, an older guy, made me feel so loved and very supported. It was weirdly almost like having another dad (calm down—he wasn't *that* old). Jack liked looking after me and I found myself looking up to him with a great deal of respect—after all, he was ten years older than me and had done a few extra laps around the sun. My relationship with him was a much more mature one. There were dinners and wines over never-ending conversations. It was here that my love for wine and good food started. The only downside to this relationship was that he had been married before and had a child. So not only did I enter into a relationship but a ready-made family too. At the ripe old age of twenty-one, I thought I was the perfect woman for the job and took to raising his daughter as I would my own (even though I was still, let's be honest, a child at heart myself). My relationship with him consisted of me loving him way more than he loved me. While he was very well established, I just worked to pay my bills and waited for the day to be over so I could be with him again. It was an uneasy place to be, and if I could go back and tell twenty-one-year-old Amy anything, it would be: *Calm your tits, girlfriend. You are coming across like a GRADE A, STAGE FIVE PSYCHOPATH. Get a hobby! One that doesn't involve Jack!* He also loved his daughter far more than I felt he ever loved me, and while I'm sure he had a place for us both in his heart, at twenty-one I couldn't stand feeling like I was second best. I added 'No baggage' to my recipe. (That might look different at the age of thirty-seven, but as a twenty-one-year-old I thought it was best to include it in my prep for the perfect man.)

Thanks to Jack breaking up with me and ruining what felt like my entire life, I impulsively booked a one-way ticket to the UK with Mum and Dad to help celebrate my grandpa's eightieth birthday, while I tried to recover from another near-death heartache. I thought, *I'll just book myself a ticket home when I get there—I might want to stay for a few weeks and do some travelling.* Maybe Jack would miss me while I was gone and declare his undying love for me. Neither eventuated. My mum had been telling me to go and live abroad and travel for years, and truth be told it had never really been that appealing. But two weeks into the trip, a girlfriend of mine reached out and said she had just moved to London and had a spare room if I wanted to rent it out and stay on for a bit. Cue two-and-a-half years of living abroad: travelling throughout Europe, partying, finding my independence (just not in the kitchen), working two jobs, living in share houses and meeting new people from all over the world.

It was here I met the married man (whom I didn't know was married at the time). He was South African and he had been playing professional rugby in the UK. His visa had expired. I met him at one of the Aussie bars in Clapham South and we hit it off instantly. He was tall, buff and very handsome. A total gentleman, too. Every night before we would go on a date, he would send flowers to my office. He was equal parts romantic and elusive—the most elusive son of a bitch I'd ever met. One minute he would be blowing up my phone and then I would have no contact with him for a week. *Play it cool, Amz,* I told myself. *You can't go all Stage Five again after saying goodbye to Jack with the bags in Sydney.*

The problem was, I'm not a lunatic, and I knew something was up. Was he potentially frigid? Maybe. Or wanting to take things super slow? Sure, I thought of that. But *married*? Never. I would go over to his house quite often. His phone was never to be seen but he would excuse himself for bathroom breaks and disappear for fifteen minutes at a time. Either the guy had IBS or there was some bullshit going down.

The last night I saw him, things got super hot and heavy in his bedroom. We hadn't actually had penetrative sex at that point—it had been almost three months, and we had done lots of other adult things, but tonight it seemed like it was go time. When push came to shove, and it was time to put P into V, he did this bizarre manoeuvre to ninja himself out of the bed and roll onto the floor. It was the weirdest turn of events, and I honestly had no idea what was going on.

Had I not showered? Was he not into me? Was he gay? So many questions—none of which I got answers to that night. I left feeling unwanted, ridiculously horny and very perplexed. For the next week there was radio silence from both of us. Then, on Saturday morning as I was leaving my place to walk to my job at the pub, a Fiat 500 literally mounted the gutter and drove straight towards me, its horn blasting, almost taking out my legs. There were screams from everyone around and then a beautiful blonde woman got out of the car. She took one look at me and charged at me like a rugby league front-rower. I'd never been in a fight before, and it turns out I'm absolutely woeful—but really great at swinging in the air and connecting with nothing. We were locked in a contest of survival of the unfittest (or maybe that was just me since moving to the UK and surviving almost solely on hot chips with salt and vinegar) and when we were eventually pulled apart, she broke down in tears, screaming, 'How could you *fuck my husband*?'

'Fuck your WHAT?'

Wait . . . was that a South African accent? Oh god. It instantly made sense. Right then and there I added 'No shady pricks' to my recipe, but I also addressed the situation with her over multiple jugs of Pimm's. I walked her all the way back to the night I met her husband and how he had only ever referred to himself as single. I've done some bad shit in my life but knowingly messing around with another woman's husband would never ever be one of them. I answered every single one of her questions, showed her text messages and receipts of our past together and told her anything she wanted to know, however painful it seemed to be for her to hear. I never ever spoke to her again but she thanked me for being so upfront and honest, and ended up apologising to me for her husband's behaviour and for almost taking me out with her car. She left looking like an enraged woman on a mission and I never cared to find out what happened to him. Dirty dog.

Not long after that, I met one of the many loves of my life. I don't believe you only ever have one true love. I believe you'll have a few along the way. Sam was one of them. I met him in a nightclub in Covent Garden. I was out with a few girlfriends and, in true Amy fashion, was carving up the dance floor without a care in the world. I'm pretty sure he bought me a drink and we hung out with his friends. I woke up with a very fuzzy memory of the night and a photo of the two of us in my camera roll. He texted me the next morning to ask me out for dinner and, as shallow as it sounds, from the photo in my camera roll I wasn't keen. He wasn't my type, although that statement is laughable because if I added a picture of each guy I'd been with, you would be left scratching your head, thinking, *WTF is her type?* But I went anyway.

That first date was the beginning of us and the end of me being single. I had lined my girlfriend up with a plausible plan to get me the fuck out of there within the first hour if he was boring as shit or I wasn't into him, but I never answered her call. Our date went for more than seven hours as we sat in a booth talking and laughing about anything and everything. He was witty, charming and hilarious, and had some of the best banter I'd ever come across. He was a few years older than me, lived with his dad and was a PE teacher. This relationship felt like the most normal relationship

I had ever had. We moved fairly quickly and after a few months I was living with him at his dad's place in Acton. We were both working adults, and the love we had for each other felt even. He made almost all of my unrealistic expectations of a relationship seem not so far-fetched after all.

A huge thing I took from this relationship for the recipe was 'Equality'—the exact thing I had been looking for—but I also found 'Friendship'. Aside from just being a wonderful boyfriend, he was the person I was closest to while living abroad with no family. He was my best friend, my family and my lover. The kicker was that he was English and I didn't want to live in England forever. We made plans to go to Sydney for Christmas—I left two weeks earlier and he was going to follow me out. During the two weeks I spent at home without him, you wouldn't believe it but 'Baggage Jack' came back on the scene . . . apparently he'd waited for me the whole time I was overseas (no word of a lie). I met up with him for a coffee like the absolute dickhead that I was.

Within the first hour I knew I was in trouble. All the feelings I had tried to bury so deeply came rushing back to the surface. I didn't want to leave the cafe. I decided I wanted to read the book of us all over again—even though I knew how each chapter ended, even though I knew it wasn't a book I should start reading again. I couldn't help it. I led with my heart.

After seeing Jack, I feared how my body was reacting. I was praying that when Sam arrived in Australia all the love I had felt for him would rush back. But I was wrong. I wanted so badly for things to be how they were before I left the UK. I had written him a letter, heartbroken at the thought of flying home without him, tearful at the thought of not having him to snuggle up to at night for two weeks. And yet there I was, standing at Sydney Airport, watching him come through the arrivals gate with a strange sense of emptiness.

Still, even now, I have no idea what happened. Had I not closed the book properly on Jack? Had I just ignored the feelings I had always had for him, and when I saw him again they'd sprouted back up? Mum said that if I had truly been in love with Sam, nothing would have changed when I met up with Jack for a coffee. But every-thing changed.

I felt sick to my stomach because I knew I was going to hurt Sam. I spent the next two weeks over Christmas trying to feel that same old love but I couldn't get there. On the day he left to go back to England, he said to me, 'You don't love me anymore . . . I can feel it. Something in your voice changed on the fourth of December, and you haven't been the same since.' That was the day I had met up with Jack.

Sometimes I think about what my life would have been like if I had just waited and come back to Australia with Sam. But I also think that everything in life happens for a reason, and every decision leads me to where I need to be. I don't carry a lot of regrets with me but I will always regret the way I hurt Sam. He didn't deserve it. It would take me years to find someone who made me feel as happy in a relationship as I had felt with him.

Two years later, things ended (again) with Jack, and I (again) went on a rampage of NOT DATING anyone and refusing to get into any kind of relationship. One of my girlfriends and I joked about how we had literally never had a one-night stand. We weren't women of the cloth; we were just in and out of relationships and hadn't ever experienced going home with a guy and then ghosting them. Or being ghosted. So we went on a girls' trip to Queensland and added 'one-night stand' to our itinerary. We met a nice bunch of New Zealand boys out at a nightclub and thought, *Perfect—they don't even live in the same country*. Our mission had begun. I'll skip past all the juicy bits because we can all guess what happened in the twelve minutes after we got back to their place, but HURRAAAAH: I had finally had a one-night stand, with a guy called James. Did it blow my socks off? No. Did it make me feel accomplished? Also no. So we said our goodbyes and I went on my merry way the next morning.

Only this wasn't going to be a one-night stand because James ended up flying to Sydney two weeks later to take me on a date (sex game so fierce, obviously) and I became his girlfriend a few weeks later. We did long distance for almost a year, which consisted of me flying to New Zealand once a month and him flying to Sydney once a month. Every time we saw each other there would be an exciting weekend with friends or with family, with holidays and trips to wineries. You name it, we packed it into every visit. The trouble with these kinds of relationships is that *they are not real life*. So, naturally, despite the fact that I had never experienced a normal, mundane week with the guy, I quit my job and moved to New Zealand.

It was only after uprooting my life that I realised my mum was right: I probably should have spent more than two days at a time with James before quitting my job and trying to assimilate over in New Zealand. Because, for me, communication is massive. Being able to talk to my partner after a long day or laugh at the total shitshow that life can be is so incredibly important to me, and what I soon realised after moving in with James is that he really had nothing to say. Almost ever. He was a very sweet guy but incredibly introverted, and in those four days a month that I had been seeing him, he had been the very best and most extroverted he could possibly be. There were also always friends or family around, so I didn't seem to notice how quiet he was. The normal midweek banter didn't exist, and the chats over dinner changed to watching TV. The silence was deafening. The relationship didn't have a strong foundation upon which it could grow and it was evident to me that I had romanticised the idea of things working so well. It had all been in my head. I gave it a little over a month before saying my goodbyes and returning to Australia, unemployed, with my tail between my legs and 'Communication' added to my recipe.

I dated a bunch of different men over the next couple of years, none of whom ever made me as happy as my relationship with Sam had. I used to say it was my karma for hurting him, but in hindsight it was all part of the process. You know how my nan said you have to kiss a bunch of frogs before you meet your prince? Well, I did a lot of kissing. I did a lot of learning and listening and observing and feeling. I also dated guys from lots of different cultures, which I absolutely loved: Russian, Lebanese, Italian, Greek, German, Swedish. I loved immersing myself in different cultures and seeing the way these guys and their families lived and ate and drank. I wanted to know what each guy stood for and what their culture was all about.

The Greek was only allowed to date me after he had already had a failed marriage with a Greek woman. The Russian was very strict with me and didn't like me wearing tight dresses to work. The German guy was someone I met on a family holiday in the Maldives. We were there over New Year's Eve and he was there with his family too. One minute I was walking around a peaceful island and the next I was skinny-dipping with Marc (who kind of looked like Arnold Schwarzenegger). We were on the island for ten days and on seven of them he left flowers on my bungalow doorstep. We held hands walking to breakfast and spent our days snorkelling and looking at coral and fish, and then making love under the stars on the beach when everyone else went to bed. He didn't speak much English, which suited me fine. I didn't really take anything from this relationship other than that it was exactly how I expected a holiday romance to feel: romantic, intense, joyful and nothing more. I felt like a character in a Mills & Boon summer romance, and I left with no feelings but a genuine appreciation of Marc for making my holiday so enjoyable.

The guy I dated before Rhian was the one who had the most profound impact on me. He had a big personality like my dad's, and if I had been more similar to Mum it would have been a truly harmonious relationship. I fell for him so hard and so fast, and I used to walk around the house giddy with what I thought was love. It was definitely lust to begin with, but the romance was incredible and I could barely wipe the cheesy grin off my face. For the first four months, I barely came up for air from our very own love bubble. However, there were red flags from the get-go, which I tried to ignore constantly. There was jealousy and insecurity, and behind every smiling photo of us there were arguments. He had a need for control and I'm not the kind of person you can control. He didn't like me going out with my friends or seeing my family. He was only happy when we were together. He had gone cold turkey off his anti-depressants and I was 'apparently' the only drug he needed. I knew things weren't right but I loved him so much, and I really wanted to believe that I could fix it.

Have you ever been with someone and felt like you were their whole world? Someone who you felt like you needed to save? He had a problem with me sleeping over at a girlfriend's place or having dinner with a friend, and he had an intense possessiveness that led him to go through my phone and read messages on my socials. He was always so suspicious but had absolutely no need to be. I was nothing but faithful and loyal to him.

I had never experienced a relationship quite like it and, even though I'm a pretty tough character, it started to have an effect on me. The fights and constant arguing—to justify going out, or wearing a certain outfit to work—were draining on my soul and, without knowing it, I started to change. Instead of fighting him on everything, I would just turn down invites to see friends. I would make up excuses to not attend work events because I just couldn't be bothered dealing with the cold shoulder I would get when I got home. I remember one night so clearly. I had been out in Kings Cross in Sydney for one of my best friends' birthdays. He had chosen not to come and had given me a list of reasons why I shouldn't go, but I was adamant that I was going. A bunch of my girlfriends were there as well as family and cousins. My girlfriend and I were standing near the bar chatting to her two male cousins who were roughly the same age as us. The next thing I knew, the bar photographer had walked past and snapped a photo of the four of us. Just standing there with drinks in our hands. To Amy in any other relationship, this wouldn't have been an issue—she wouldn't have thought twice about it. But to Amy in the current relationship, this was bad. Diabolical even. Because even though I wasn't doing a single thing wrong, my boyfriend had a way of inducing so much anxiety in me. I ended up running through the nightclub desperately searching for the photographer and asking him to delete the picture out of fear that my boyfriend would see it and make his own twisted assumptions up over it. It was so out of character for me, I remember my girlfriend turning to me and saying, 'Look what he's done to you, you haven't done a single thing wrong and yet you are so on edge, Amy.'

I could absolutely have stayed with him, and I have a few girlfriends who have done so in these kinds of relationships. The love they feel overrules any common sense they have, and they just push their doubts to the back of their mind. When things were good with him they were absolutely incredible, but when they were bad they were really bad. I just knew that, regardless of how much I loved him, I would never have felt comfortable bringing children into a relationship that was so volatile and toxic at times. In any close, loving relationship it's so important to find the right balance of personal freedom and commitment. When two people can be together in a way that respects each person's individual space and at the same time expresses unequivocal commitment, then both people can relax and be who they are. 'Freedom' is so important to me in the relationship recipe, but in that one I had none of it.

I moved into the city after leaving that relationship, shed multiple kilos and partied my ass off to try to numb the pain of having left him. Even though I knew I had made the right decision, it hurt like hell. I moved in with a girlfriend and had a glorious summer swimming down at Redleaf Beach in Double Bay, doing face masks and eating pizza on the floor of our lounge room before going out for a dance. I reluctantly got back onto the dating scene, but my last relationship had made me put up some pretty aggressive walls. If a guy gave me even a slight indication of being a bit possessive, I bounced. I dated some really nice guys, but my heart wasn't with any of them.

The way I met Rhian was equal parts cheesy and what I like to call fate. I remember lying on my bed one day, scrolling through the Instagram Explore page for something different. I came across a photo of a guy with dark features and blue eyes lying in the middle of two French bulldogs. His picture immediately caught my eye, and when I clicked on it his profile was set to public, so naturally I had a stalk of his photos. I couldn't work out if there was a girlfriend on the scene or not, so I gave the dog pic a double tap and got on with my day.

Five minutes later, the guy sent me a message: 'hey @amzlc001 [my old Instagram handle], you're cute, what brings you to my page?'

I thought it was a bit cringe, but wrote back something about his dogs being cute. He asked if he could take me on a date and promised he would bring the dogs. It felt a little desperate, so I didn't reply. Cold, I know. We followed each other and chucked a few likes at each other, but I didn't think anything more of him beyond his cute dogs.

A few months later I was walking across Pitt Street to grab myself a coffee and I saw a tall, dark, handsome man walking towards me. I instantly recognised him but couldn't remember exactly where I knew him from. We walked straight past each other and then I kind of turned around. Luckily, he also turned around. Thank god one of us knew the other's name (hint, it wasn't me) and he said, 'Amy?' I of course pretended like I knew exactly who he was, so we stopped for a chat. He was charming and had a great aura about him, and big blue sparkly eyes. But I still couldn't place him. I walked away from our brief conversation feeling a little bit puzzled, but fortunately he messaged me almost immediately on Instagram to say it had been nice to bump into me. It was him—the French bulldog guy.

We lined up a date for that night and went out for dinner and drinks. It was one of the best first dates I've ever been on and I even messaged him that after he had dropped me home. Zero chill. Rhian loves telling the story to anyone who will listen that he took me on the best date of my life. Our chemistry was palpable, and he had an energy that matched mine. I am pretty full of life, a glass-half-full type of girl who genuinely finds the positives in most situations, and it was nice to meet someone who was on the same level. He was so much fun to be around and our initial dating period was so exciting.

Night noodle markets, late-night rides on the back of his motorbike to go and sit under the stars at Bondi, pizza and wine on the beach while the sun went down, trips down south, homecooked meals, movies, and meeting each other's friends and family.

While I will be the first to admit that I fell for him pretty quickly, we were both incredibly cautious to begin with. First, it took me a month to realise his name was pronounced like 'Ryan'. I had been telling all my friends and family that I had met a guy called 'Rhee-arn' and because it's quite an unusual name for a man, everyone started to speculate about whether he was Welsh. I assumed yes, so for a solid month I told people I was dating 'Rhee-arn the Welsh guy'. Turns out it's just Ryan spelled 'Rhian'.

There was also the fact that Rhian had just gotten out of a nine-year relationship, and when we met he was penetrating anything with a heartbeat to make up for lost time. After coming out of my own particularly traumatic relationship, I didn't want to settle down with just anyone, so the two of us played this weird stoical game to begin with, with neither of us wanting to be the first person to give into our feelings.

After we'd been dating for five weeks, there was a slight miscommunication about whether or not we were exclusive. Once we'd sorted that out, we had a long and open-ended conversation in which Rhian bared all the skeletons in his closet to me and we both laid down some ground rules: what we expected from each other in a relationship, and what our non-negotiables were. Things were playing out exactly as I wanted them to. So much give and take. Very 50/50. Much equality. After six weeks, it felt like our relationship was in fast-forward mode. We both let our walls down and went all-in.

I'm not saying I brought my toothbrush over straight away and did a poo while he showered next to me, although I may have found a permanent spot for my toothbrush and held conversations with him while he showered and I released my bowels. By month three he asked me if I wanted to go to America with him and, being the spontaneous human that I am, I thought, *Why not?* Let's just say thank fucken god I did because little did we know that it would be the only international holiday we would ever go on alone. We spent three weeks in the US, in San Francisco and Santa Barbara and LA, and then flew over to Mexico and did Playa del Carmen and Tulum, and drank at least four hundred and eighty margaritas in ten days. It honestly felt like a honeymoon—just the two of us in our 'honeymoon period', doing the things we absolutely love the most. Eating, drinking, skinny-dipping in the ocean under the stars, swimming all day, taking naps entwined in each other's arms and making love frequently.

While a few of my ex-partners had loved how outgoing and confident I was when they met me, it was the one thing about me that they would always try to change once we were dating. But Rhian saw my flame and always let it burn. Sometimes he'd even throw petrol on it to help me burn brighter! He loved me for me and encouraged me to always be myself. I remember being in Playa del Carmen and we went to Coco Bongo (IYKYK). I can't think of many boyfriends who would encourage me to get up on stage in front of three hundred people and dance on the bar while having tequila poured down my throat by Mexican men, but Rhian did. He was there clapping me on from the sidelines. He has been my biggest cheerleader in life from the beginning, and it's an incredible place to be in a relationship. He has always loved me for who I am.

The first thing that stood out to me about our relationship was how 'at home' I felt in his presence. I once had a boyfriend who I wouldn't even let see me without make-up. I would set my alarm for some ungodly hour and make sure I was up before the sun to apply an entirely new face. Yet here I was showering with Rhian, drooling on his pillow and probably snoring like a hibernating bear. (He will *love* reading this chapter.)

When people ask where your home is, you often name a suburb or town. But it felt like Rhian was my home. Home is simply where you are wanted, loved and appreciated, and I felt all of those things. It is where you're good enough, even with every flaw. It is someone giving you a reason to stay, and I wanted to stay with him. He made me feel secure, and he made me feel seen.

Rhian also made life fun. He very simply eased every worry I had just by standing next to me. It didn't matter what I was going through because he was there—and I had never been one to depend on anyone before. He was there whether I was glammed up to the nines or looking like Hagrid from Harry Potter off the back of a three-day bender. He loved me and all forty-five of my different looks. I also quickly realised that when I went out, I would have more fun *with* him there than without. We loved eating out and trying new restaurants. He would be up on the dance floor with me at every wedding. We could sit on the beach and chat for hours. He quickly became so much more than my boyfriend—he was my friend, my confidant, the person I could tell all of my darkest fears and secrets to. He's never once tried to dim my sparkle. He still encourages me to be myself on the daily, regardless of how rogue that self can sometimes go. He knows if there's music playing somewhere in the distance, I will sniff it out faster than a beagle at the airport and he will lose me for hours on a dance floor.

In terms of my metaphorical recipe, Rhian ticked off so many things that were important to me: he's family oriented, and offers me equality, friendship, communication and freedom. He lets me breathe and loves me unconditionally. He's also not a shady prick and he doesn't have any past children. (That we know about.)

The long roller-coaster ride that I jumped on as a teen and eventually got off when I was thirty-one took me to some of my biggest highs and lowest lows. It was exciting and traumatic as it twisted and turned, but for every hard relationship there were loads of good ones. Those relationships taught me a lot about myself: what I can handle, what I enjoy most and what I absolutely will not stand for. If I could go back in time, would I want my youthful expectations to become a reality? Absolutely not. I wouldn't have travelled or met the people I met. I'm so glad the I rode the ride for as long as I did, because it led me to Rhian and a love that is constantly evolving. It swells and dwindles and softens and intensifies. It won't always be the way it was when we first met, but he was the first guy I ever wanted to jump on the marriage roller-coaster with, and hold on to tight.

SONG LISTS FOR THE LOVESICK PUPPY

Here is a collection of songs I bust out at HIGH VOLUME in my car when I'm deep in the honeymoon stage of a relationship. Just kidding—I sing these all year round. Even seven years into a marriage. I have two editions, organised by era.

1960s–2000s Love Song edition

- 'I Will Always Love You'—Dolly Parton or Whitney Houston
- 'Can't Help Falling in Love'—Elvis Presley, or UB40's version
- 'God Only Knows'—The Beach Boys
- 'Unchained Melody'—The Righteous Brothers
- 'When a Man Loves a Woman'—Percy Sledge
- 'Always'—Bon Jovi
- 'Perhaps Love'—John Denver and Plácido Domingo (my dad and I used to dance around the lounge room to this; the lyrics are so beautiful)
- 'My Girl'—The Temptations (my dad and I danced to this at my wedding)
- 'Somethin' Stupid'—Frank Sinatra and Nancy Sinatra
- 'You Needed Me'—Anne Murray
- 'I'll Stand by You'—The Pretenders
- 'Back for Good'—Take That
- 'Glory of Love'—Peter Cetera
- 'All My Life'—K-Ci & JoJo (I went through my high school relationships with this on repeat)

1990s and Beyond Love Song edition

- 'All of Me'—John Legend
- 'A Thousand Years'—Christina Perri
- 'This Year's Love'—David Gray
- 'Iris'—Goo Goo Dolls
- 'Stay'—Rihanna ft. Mikky Ekko
- 'Beyond'—Leon Bridges
- 'Without You'—Mariah Carey
- 'Lay Me Down'—Sam Smith
- 'I'll Make Love To You'—Boyz II Men (I sing this to a tray of Mars Bar slice after it's firmed up)
- 'Shallow'—Lady Gaga and Bradley Cooper
- 'If I Ain't Got You'—Alicia Keys
- 'Until I Found You'—Stephen Sanchez
- 'Always Be My Baby'—Mariah Carey

LOVE

A list of twenty things that I have loved for a period, if not all thirty-seven years, of my life.

1. The sunrise—if you can manage to get up in time for it.
2. The sunset, more so when there is a little cloud coverage and all the soft auburn colours light up the sky and hide behind the outline of the clouds, teasing you with a subtle light show.
3. The way the first sip of coffee tastes.
4. ORGASMS. I love the way my face goes a little numb and I get pins and needles in it. My toes curl slightly and for a brief six seconds there is no greater feeling on earth. God damn, I want one *right now*.
5. R&B music and the way it makes me want to move my hips. I used to go out dancing from 10 p.m. until the sun came up, drug- and alcohol-free too. I could just dance and dance and dance. These days I need to take an anti-inflammatory beforehand and rub some Voltaren on these hips to loosen them up before leaving home, but my love for dance will *never ever* die. I'll be swinging around on my walking frame in the aged care facility, still attempting to drop it like it's hot. Watch this space.
6. The way exercise makes me feel. Like I genuinely fucken LOVE what it does to my body, even though I hate exercise more than I hate it when my husband finishes in twenty-five seconds. I am one of those annoying bitches

who likes to tell *everyone* who will listen that I've just exercised and how great I feel. Not a single person ever asks, but I'm writing that shit in the sky or standing on the side of the street happy-clapping in my activewear.

7. Self-pleasure. I love watching porn. Lesbian porn, in fact. You should watch it. Girls know how to do that thing you like.

8. The first shower you have after spending the day at the beach, and how clean and warm and sun-kissed your skin feels.

9. Christmas time. I might have married the Grinch but there is enough Christmas cheer in me to make up for Rhian's lack of enthusiasm.

10. Watching my kids sleep. Not because that's when they are at their most well-behaved—but also that too. I love how peaceful and serene and angelic they look.

11. Listening to my mum play the piano while I lay upstairs in my bed as a kid.

12. Warm tropical climates. Don't ask me to come to the snow with you—there's nothing I hate more than being cold.

13. How much heat Rhian generates. He is like an electric blanket at night-time and he always lets me warm up my freezing-cold feet on him.

14. Living without inhibitions. Took me thirty-plus years to get here but man, does it feel good. The minute you

stop caring about what other people think, your soul does some funky shit and you feel on top of the world.

15. Negronis. The first time I tried one I'm pretty sure I used the words 'petrol' and 'grass' to describe it to a friend, but they are my most sought-after drink when I head out. (But only one or two of them, because they are potent as hell.)

16. Getting into bed after I've changed the sheets. But only linen or bamboo sheets. Clean, cool and fresh. Ohhhh yeah.

17. Smiling at everybody I walk past, even when they do a double take because they are confused about why I'm smiling at them. I don't break out into a toothy serial-killer grin—just a small smile, as if to say 'Morning' or 'Evening' as I'm walking past.

18. Playing with hair, so much so that you'll always find me running my fingers through the hair of whoever is sitting next to me. It only got weird once: I was out for lunch with a senior lawyer after starting a job two weeks before, and I accidentally started running my fingers through her hair. We've since worked out I have sensory issues.

19. Perfumes. My most favourite thing ever on a man is when he smells good. That, and good oral hygiene.

20. Making people laugh, be it with me or at me. Laughter is the best medicine in the world.

PREGNANCY

Expectation: I am a beautiful goddess, glowing effortlessly, cherishing every moment

Reality: Equal parts human, cow and something that lives under a bridge

I grew up with a maternal gene peacocking out in the forefront. *Who wants me to hold their baby?* If anyone had a doll, baby or Barbie lying around, I would be mothering it. If your little brother wanted to play with us but you just wanted to hang out with kids your own age, I'd mother him. When we had family friends come over and they had a child smaller than myself, I would be mothering that child. I would stuff pillows under all my tops and dresses and pretend to be nine months pregnant.

I was going to have six kids. I had all their names written down in my diary from the age of twelve. They'd all be two years apart, so I'd be pregnant or breastfeeding for almost twelve years straight. NO PROBLEMO. I'd be the *best* mum (just ask me). Whenever I saw a pregnant woman I would stare in fascination, imagining how there was one of me growing inside her tummy—a real human who would start off small and soon be walking on its own legs and using public transport. Honestly, the female body is an absolute gift.

My mum always told me she absolutely loved being pregnant. I used to flick through old photos of her with her cute little basketball bump and killer pins, and dream about the day that I could be pregnant. I would ask Mum what it was like being pregnant and she always said it was the best feeling in the world.

'And how do you get the baby out?' I would ask her, with inquisitive eyes.

'It's just like doing the biggest poo you've ever done,' Mum would always say.

As a kid who ate *a lot* of carbs and red meat, I knew all about dropping off huge turds—and the occasional anal fissure—so I already knew I had this in the bag. *I couldn't wait!*

Fast-forward to the year 2014. Where do I start? If only an anal fissure was the worst it was going to get.

Let me start by saying that not all people are going to like what I write about pregnancy, but the beauty of this being a book is that you can just skip to the next chapter and pretend this one doesn't exist. Because I need to unleash some not-so-pleasant stories about carrying a fetus—some cold hard facts from my own lived experience.

I know I should be grateful that my body allowed me to get pregnant in the first place. I know every bastard star in the universe has to align, and your body temperature has to be 36.2 degrees and rise at exactly the right time, and you have to be facing the Milky Way while doing it doggy style with Lionel Richie playing in the background. I know it's hard to fall pregnant. And I truly am grateful. I know there are so many women out there who would long to experience the absolute shitshow that I'm about to write about. But, while I do acknowledge that I am lucky to even tell these stories, I've always been a speaker of my own truths—an oversharer, if you will—and I won't be sugar-coating how much of a daily struggle I had carrying my three babies.

I'll start with my first. I remember going to lunch in the city and one of my girlfriends gathered us around her to tell us that she had recently discovered she was pregnant. HURRAH! None of us were getting any younger and how much more partying could we do? It seemed like the perfect time. We all squealed with delight like teenagers getting ready for their first Blue Light Disco and engulfed her in those excited hugs you give when one of your posse is about to procreate. I remember listening intently to her as she told us the story about her period being late and how she just *felt* different. I remember my ears pricking up and instantly realising that my period was also late. I also had a dull ache in my left-hand side but assumed it was my impending period. I was only late by a day. *Don't stress, Amy*, I thought, mentally checking myself.

But as I walked back to work, I called said pregnant friend and said something along the lines of, 'Ohhhh, I think I'm late too. Imagine if I was pregnant with you!' We laughed it off because Rhian and I had only been dating for six months and I didn't even know for sure he wasn't a serial killer at that point. But something was telling me to go and buy a pregnancy test. *Go on, Amy, just go and do one for fun*, I told myself. But another part of me wondered what on earth I was doing. It was like I was having an out-of-body experience and my conscious brain was just going along for the ride.

Back at the office, I sat inside a toilet cubicle and peed on the stick. Three minutes later and whaddya know . . . my egg had been fertilised. WHAT THE FUCK. I had drunk at least twelve vodka sodas on the weekend. I instantly felt like I was going to black out. Sweat surged over my entire body and my hearing felt like it switched off. I know this feeling well. If I had been standing, this would have been the part where I face-planted into the cubicle wall and slid down it, but because I was already sitting with my pants around my ankles I kind of just leaned to the side and waited for the wave to past.

Naturally the first thing I did was text my girlfriend a photo of the positive pregnancy test. Pretty sure her reply was something really beautiful like 'GET FUCKED' and then she tried to call me, while I screened her call and tried to gather my thoughts. *I love babies. What if Rhian doesn't? How did the swimmer get through? What am I going to do?* I didn't even know Rhian's middle name but I knew I really loved him. We were balls deep in our honeymoon era but we also weren't getting any younger.

I made the stupid decision to call my mum first (never mind the baby's daddy) and I should have known how she would react. You remember how I used to peacock with the maternal gene— well, where do you think I got it from? We are talking about the English Mother Teresa here, the woman who loves babies more than anything else in the world, and I've rung to tell her I've just found out I'm pregnant. She screamed like she had just won a free cruise and then started heavy panting as it sank in that she was going to be a grandma. All before she had even asked me how I was feeling. I'm almost certain I could have procreated with a wombat and she would have been ecstatic. Her excitement definitely rubbed off on me, and I told her she was crazy and that I should probably have a chat to Rhian about the news before she ran out and bought me a Bugaboo pram.

Most people would wait till work was over and have a face-to-face but I'm also the most impatient person in the world. So I just sent Rhian a picture of the positive test result, then waited for the panic to kick in on his side of the phone.

The call came. The panic did not. In its place was a little bit of uncertainty and a lot of excitement.

I honestly wasn't sure what to expect, so I had answered the phone with an open mind. But I truly wasn't ready for him to be so onboard with us starting a family so soon. Had my mum already called him and peer-pressured him in to answering this way? My hesitation and worry melted away within the first couple of minutes of us being on the phone because the truth of the matter was that I really didn't want to end the pregnancy. I knew deep down in my soul of souls that Rhian was my penguin. He was the man I was meant to be with, and had this scenario played out with anyone else I don't think I would have felt the way I felt. Hearing his excitement over the phone made me fall in love with him even more, and I hung up feeling giddy and excited. I was also nervous as hell: I had just started a new job about nine weeks before, so my pregnancy (if viable) was going to go down like a lead balloon.

By week five, I was acutely aware I was pregnant. I was hungrier than an entire rugby league team after intensive high-altitude training. No amount of food could satisfy me, it seemed. Eating was also the only thing that helped with my now constant nausea. I wasn't a morning spewer or night-time spewer. I was a 24/7, nauseous-as-hell, 'Am I going to spew, am I not going to spew?' mess of a woman who basically survived on *carbs only.* Now I'm not sure if this was a placebo thing, where I kind of just told my brain, *Hey, guess what? We're pregnant now, babes! GREEN LIGHT TO BULK UP!* or whether I actually needed to eat that much to help with the nausea, but I didn't really give it much thought. I just ate and ate and did what I needed to do. I was in beast mode and I was always hangry. Meat pies for breakfast, hot chips for morning tea, chicken schnitzel roll for a second morning tea . . . you get the gist.

When I wasn't eating I was trying to sleep. On my lunch breaks. On the floor in meeting rooms. I was deliriously tired. I envy the women who have no appetite and don't even notice a difference when they are pregnant because I felt like the walking dead. My thighs expanded at the speed of light. They clapped me on wherever I went. My boobs went from a 10D to a 12H and my damn milk hadn't even come in yet. I looked like the zombie version of Dolly Parton—the one who hasn't slept in years but is on the hunt for some fast food, with her huge bazookas leading the way. My hormones fluctuated between making me cry at NRMA commercials and making me want to fight people who wouldn't say thanks when I let them into traffic.

By twelve weeks, when most people tell their friends and family, I looked like I was already halfway to giving birth. My face had started to blend into my chest and I had burst capillaries that looked like hickeys all over my breasts. My gums would bleed every morning and if I didn't make breakfast my number-one priority when waking up, I would spew almost instantly. I would catch the bus to work every morning and have nosebleeds on almost every ride. I'm certain people on the bus were trying to work out whether I was some sort of street-working meth head with boob hickeys or just a pregnant woman having a rough time. There was a definite glow about me, but it was either from my face skin being stretched out thanks to the 15 kilos I had already gained, or all the grease from the Maccas I was eating. There was nothing ethereal and glowy about me—nah, definitely missed out on that. I will tell you what I *did* get that I didn't see coming, though.

HORNY.

Yep. I found it weird too, but in the second trimester I carried on like a sixteen-year-old boy who has discovered porn and how to jerk his pork sword. I would say that I've always had a pretty high sex drive, and have always been keen to explore new things and go skinny-dipping on the beach. But this pregnancy did some weird things to my hornbag levels. If there was a lounge chair, I'd be straddling it. It was like my clit had taken a pinger and every single molecule on the outside layer of it was peaking.

Fast-forward to me at nineteen weeks, when the nausea had died down. I was still eating like a front-rower and I'd started looking more like a rectangle than a human and all of a sudden I was the toey-est human on earth. Poor Rhian couldn't escape. But he'd done this to me, so when the silverback gorilla (me) came looking for some action, you'd best believe he had to oblige. It was a hundred per cent consensual, might I add; we just had to very quickly work out the best positions to do it in to ensure zombie Dolly Parton wasn't suffocating him and everyone could hit a home run.

By the third trimester, I had gained almost 30 kilos. Was it a big baby? Was it the hot chips I'd eaten twice a day for eight months? The answer is irrelevant, if you ask me. My undercarriage felt like it was carrying a Mazda3 inside of it, my areolas had stretched to the size of digestive biscuits and I had started to do the waddle. Driving was hard. Sleeping was all but impossible, and my levels of comfort were sitting at well below zero. I was still always hungry but had to eat tiny meals for ants because it felt like all the room in my stomach was being rented out by a small fetus and there was nowhere for the food to go. Cue the most horrendous heartburn of all time. Every night at 7 p.m. it would start, and I had to sleep upright on five different pillows to ensure my oesophagus didn't have a raging forest fire going on inside it. I remember going in for a check-up with a midwife at thirty-four weeks and I was measuring almost thirty-nine weeks. That's how large my stomach was—apparently five weeks ahead. I was sent for a scan, then and there, and they were able to work out that the reason I could barely breathe when sitting upright was because I had a fun little thing called polyhydramnios—excess fluid in my uterus—which was fine for bub but made things extremely uncomfortable for the waddling oven on legs. It's also the reason that my waters exploded at thirty-seven weeks . . . but I'll save that part for the birthing chapter.

My second pregnancy was so very different. Like chalk and cheese. I should add that I didn't find out the sex of any of my kids before they were born—they were all surprises—but my second pregnancy with Bobby felt so different that I knew, almost instantly, that this baby would be the opposite sex to Charli, my first.

This time, I felt depressed throughout the first trimester. I felt like I had a dark cloud of heaviness hanging over me at all times and I couldn't shake it. I didn't realise at the time that perinatal depression is a real thing and I am sure I experienced it. I would wake up most days and slap on a happy face for my daughter's sake but the truth was that all I felt like doing was crying. As I've mentioned, I have always been a glass-half-full type of girl who can always find the positives in any situation, so feeling this way knocked me right out of my comfort zone. Most days I would wait for Charli's nap time and then, as soon as she was down, I would sit on the couch and unleash the tears. It was almost therapeutic getting them out but at the same time I knew something wasn't right.

I started to talk to girlfriends who suggested I go and see someone, and I ended up talking to one of the midwives in my midwifery group. She put me in touch with an incredibly beautiful GP, and together we worked on a game plan: if I still felt the same way come the middle of my second trimester, we would look into some different types of medications. But, at around fourteen weeks, the fog seemed to shift and I felt like I could breathe easy again.

Where I was large and kind of glowy (thanks to Maccas grease) with my first pregnancy, in my second I was dry and covered in dermatitis, and had grown at least thirty-six new skin tags. I'm not joking: those little fleshy pieces of extra skin littered my body—in my armpits, on my butthole, and a huge one on one of my lady bits, which we affectionately named Norma. My breasts looked like raging volcanoes, with red and blue veins bulging out everywhere. I remember trying to trim my pubes because I was off to get a spray tan for a wedding and you can't tan a yeti . . . but as I was standing in front of the mirror I realised I now had chin hairs. Quite the catch, I know!

Everything was itchy, but not like a normal, your-skin-is-stretching-out-to-make-room-for-your-next-baby type of itchy. I mean I would wake in the middle of the night and find any sort of weapon (hairbrush, nail file, even forks from the cutlery drawer) and scratch the bottom of my feet and the palms of my hands until they bled. I never got the linea nigra line—you know, the dark line of skin that starts from your belly button and goes down to your pubic area—but what I did get in its place was a line of hair that looked like an extension of my pubes, all the way up to my belly button—a belly button that looked like a turkey timer sticking out. My plumbing was all over the place, too. Some weeks I couldn't poo to save my life, and the next week my sphincter would be super relaxed and on holidays, and I would start to consider adult nappies.

The only thing that was more of a roller-coaster than what was going on with my lady parts was my hormones. SWEET BABY JESUS, WAS I A PSYCHO. I hated Rhian from the minute I found out I was pregnant again; the poor guy went from having a horny silverback gorilla as a wife to a walking skin tag who would breathe fire if he so much as came home from lunch having eaten red onion. I really didn't want to be that way. But the hormones made me. I also farted more during that pregnancy than I have ever done in my entire life, so there's that too. Oh, and the desire to even want to be in the same room as Rhian's penis, let alone near it nude, was slim to don't-fucken-touch-me. We had sex twice while I was pregnant and by the end of a long-ass nine months he was in a de facto relationship with his hand.

I went in for my thirty-eight-week check-up and I was furious. Having given birth to Charli at thirty-seven weeks, I was adamant I was going to do the same again and was super annoyed when this kid didn't seem to want to make a grand entrance as early as his sister. How dare he refuse to vacate my insides at thirty-seven weeks! I remember bitching to my midwife about how hard it was to sleep and that I was going to the toilet at thirty-eight-minute intervals, and when she asked me if there was anything else peculiar about my pregnancy I told her that my friends and I were going to tie dental floss around Norma. Aside from the fact that my pubes seemed to be growing up my belly, the only other thing I thought was strange was the uncontrollable itching that would occur at night-time on the inside of my hands and the bottom of my feet, keeping me up for most of the dark hours.

She kind of stopped in her tracks, turned to me and asked why I hadn't mentioned this sooner. I sarcastically told her that I thought it was just another joyful symptom of pregnancy. She sent me immediately to get my bloodwork done and the following day I received a call from the obstetrician working at the hospital to tell me I had obstetric cholestasis—a build-up of the levels of bile acid in my blood. It's a royal pain in the ass for the mum but it can be quite dangerous for the unborn child if the bile acids should ever cross over into the placenta. He mentioned my levels were incredibly high (no wonder I'd almost sawn off my own hands the night before), and that I needed to come into the hospital right now so we could get the baby out. My birthing chapter will tell you all about how my first induction went. Yes, I'm clickbaiting you.

My third pregnancy . . . okay, I swear I'm not trying to drag this whole life-giving process through the mud, but WOW. If my first two weren't tough enough, my third deadset almost killed me. I will lead with: the pregnancy itself wasn't great but having to parent two toddlers while feeling like I wanted to vomit every three minutes was the real killer. I remember not being able to get off the couch at nine weeks. I looked like Big Foot's dick, I hadn't washed my hair in a fortnight, I'm not even sure if I had showered and I just felt so utterly helpless. I kept thinking to myself, *How on earth am I going to do this? How does one survive? I can't even fathom taking my clothes off to shower and yet I'm meant to turn up and parent a fourteen-month-old and an almost-three-year-old?*

I've never wanted to slip into a six-month coma more than I did during that pregnancy.

One of my many life mottos is: try to find humour in the darkest of times. You need to be able to have a laugh at the absolute pandemonium that your life can be when you are pregnant. Or when you are a mum. Or when you are just living through a super overwhelming period. Laughter is imperative, so I used to write all about my third pregnancy as a way of not going insane and to make other women feel less alone. Reading those posts now triggers me! I felt so incredibly overwhelmed and beyond exhausted. I felt like I had been pregnant or breastfeeding for sixty years by this stage. My body had gone from a size eight to the size of a Tellytubby, then back down and up again. My titties had started out cute, with nipples that would make eye contact with you, then went up to the Dolly Parton 12Hs, back down to a small handful, up to a pumping milk bar and then down to flattened road cones . . . and now they were on the incline again. I was more areola than tit and you could direct low-flying aeroplanes with my permanently erect nipples. But I knew that by the time I was done breastfeeding this third kid, I would be able to fling them up around my shoulders and use them as travel pillows—so there was a silver lining in there somewhere!

All of my scans kept telling me that this third unit was measuring in the hundredth percentile. For those of you who haven't had babies, you get scans while pregnant to measure and assess fetal growth. It's one of the main aims of antenatal care, as size and growth trajectories are important indicators of underlying fetal health. For a comparison, Charli was consistently in the fortieth percentile and Bobby was in the fiftieth percentile. My midwives assumed that I would have gestational diabetes (I didn't) because they couldn't work out why my third baby was so big compared to my first two. The legs, arms, head, you name it—it was all off the charts. 'At least bub is in proportion,' they would say, to try to soften the blow. *Cool cool*, I thought, *but I'm really not keen on being ripped from here to China, so how quickly can we evacuate this one?* The pressure between my legs had escalated to an excruciating level. It felt like I had a 9-kilo bowling ball inside of me and every time I stood up or tried to walk anywhere it crushed into my organs threating to prolapse every part of my insides. I've never waddled so hard as I did in those last three months.

A vivid memory I have of that blissful time (and one that my mum loves to remind me about) is when I sat in front of the mirror to trim my crotch beard. I was Dumbledore by the end of that pregnancy, and I had lined up a birth photographer for my final birth—and no one wants a crowning photo that's mostly covered by a Belanglo State Forest of pubes. So, there I was, whipper-snippering away, when the beard finally parted and there it was: my huge purple vagina. I'm not talking a shade of lilac either. Because of the abovementioned pressure, everything was a deep, dark purple. I was Barney the Dinosaur. But, worse than that, I was *sure* there were things hanging out.

Had I actually prolapsed?

ALREADY?

Was that the placenta?

Some innards?

Possibly a baby's finger or maybe just another skin tag?

I rang my mum in a panic and made her FaceTime me—a call I'm sure she would much rather forget. If I can give you any advice in this book—and I'll scatter some Amy wisdom throughout it, even though you didn't ask—NEVER VENTURE DOWN SOUTH AFTER THE EIGHT-MONTH MARK. (But if you absolutely have to, and plan on having a natural birth, lob some evening primrose oil capsules up the glory hole while you are visiting. It's sensational for softly lubing up all the muscles and softening your cervix. Sperm also works, and is probably half the reason why Charli came early . . . lol.)

Restless legs took hold of me around the six-month mark and got progressively worse each and every day. By eight months I would spend most nights horizontally moonwalking in bed and I wasn't sure what was going to kill me first: lack of sleep, the heartburn that I was certain had melted apart my chest cavity, or my pelvis that felt like it had been shattered into a million pieces. I had to eat like a Victoria's Secret model ahead of a runway show because anything more than a mouthful would come burning out of me like hot lava. The weekly scans kept reassuring me that, yes, I did in fact still have a watermelon disguised as a baby growing inside me, and the kicks were so aggressive that I reckon if said baby had just broken out of its sac and stretched out its limbs, it could have started to control my own arms and legs. The comments I made to Rhian went along the lines of:

'I can't breathe. My lungs can't even expand.'

'I can't even look at food. My stomach has been pushed up into my throat.'

'Can you shave my legs? And don't stare at Barney *or* Norma.'

'Can we look into getting a urine catheter so I can sleep for more than thirty-eight minutes at a time?'

'I just want to die.'

I had gained 19 kilos, was up four bra sizes, had consumed at the very minimum two hundred and sixty-eight Bondi burgers from Oporto (minus the chilli because heartburn). I had cried at least nine times, gained a whopping thirty-four more skin tags and only let Rhian's pork sword near me once in nine months. I ate ice cream at least thirty-five times even though I knew I was going to cop hectic reflux. (Worth it.) I lodged approximately 128,547 evening primrose oil capsules inside me to prepare for birthing a baby the size of a three-year-old. Had roughly forty baths, received an accidental stretch-and-sweep via Bobby's foot when I had a bath with him, and received three stretch-and-sweeps by trained professionals. Spent about two hundred and thirty hours watching Rhian sleep while I couldn't, and thought about punching him in the face two hundred and thirty times. I plucked sixty-four chin hairs, clipped the Dumbledore beard three times and slept roughly eighteen hours in total after finding out I was pregnant. Pretty sure I swore at the kids 2397 times and zero of those times did I regret it. I took about two hundred and fifty naps throughout the pregnancy, and only thought I was in pre-labour about a hundred and fifty times before the big day finally arrived. I went in for a scan at thirty-seven weeks and five days and they said my cervix was 'favourable' and I was already three centimetres dilated. I would be induced with the big bopper the next day, they said, and I honestly could not have done

one single day more when they told me that. I had completely and utterly lost myself in the pregnancy. I just needed the baby out.

To wrap this chapter up so that I don't sound like a totally ungrateful beast, I will say this: pregnancy will be different for every woman. Some women will be unicorns who love it and have zero complications. Others will have hyperemesis gravidarum, and those women are the true superheroes out there. And others will be somewhere in the middle, nodding their heads and understanding the hardship. The fact of the matter is, it's *hard*. It's so incredibly hard. It's taxing on our bodies, on our mental health and on our everyday lives from start to finish.

Pregnancy was absolutely *nothing* like I expected it would be and yet, once the babies were out, the everlasting changes it had brought to my body and my confidence were truly priceless. Never have I felt more womanly, soft in all the right places and firm where I need to be (excluding my undercarriage, because that had basically fallen out of me and was sweeping the floor after my third child). But there is so much empowerment in knowing that you are creating life. It's really something else.

So I want to just acknowledge that I think women are truly the most incredible humans. Whether you have been putting your body through the ringer trying to fall pregnant with fertility drugs or you have had a heinous pregnancy, there truly is no one on earth who is stronger than a woman. I have so much respect for us. For our bodies. For our minds and what we endure. My dream in life is to one day be a doula or some kind of support person for women going through pregnancy and birth because, even though it absolutely ripped my identity from me and—holy hell—almost killed me in the process, it made me a far stronger woman afterwards.

I also want to acknowledge that this chapter might have been hard for some of you out there to read. If you are one of them, I am sorry. Feel free to throw me an uppercut in the street if you are walking past me. I will take it and give you a hug in return. I really do wish for any woman out there trying for a baby to get their happy ending. If you are going through a tough time trying to conceive, the only thing I can say is to lean into the support, talk openly to friends and family, accept the help and the offers to take your mind off things when you can, and try not to lose hope. I also feel like this advice is incredibly unsolicited so I'm going to just give myself an uppercut now. Sending you all so much love and so many kisses from these pages, all sprinkled with super-magical baby dust and a huge hug for whoever needs it most.

NIGHTS OUT AS A MUM

Expectation: Dance floors are swapped for civilised lunches and no one is out past 9 p.m.

Reality: NOBODY KEEPS AMY OFF A DANCE FLOOR

Ever since I was sixteen years old and got hold of a fake ID (sorry, Dad) I have loved socialising. I'm what they call an extroverted introvert. I truly *love* my own company and crave being alone for a good chunk of my week, but then there's this other side of me that is addicted to socialising.

I love the buzz. The outfits. The free-flowing conversation. The laughing. I love music and I love the dance floor. I have never considered myself a good dancer but there is something about music that lights up my soul. My hips just take over and have a mind of their own. '*Whoa,*' I hear you ask, 'is that Shakira or Beyoncé on the dance floor?' No, it's just me, absolutely feeling myself, the beat and the energy of the music. I use music in my everyday life. It turns a frown upside down. It instantly makes me feel better.

Before kids, there would be music in my room as I got ready to go to school, or to the formal, or to go out with the girls. During labour it helped (only with my second birth, let's be honest). When my kids were babies, I would play certain songs to them that would instantly soothe them. Music makes for a great buffer when everyone is self-combusting around dinnertime and you need to throw up a distraction or just lighten the mood. They say music is the language of the soul, penetrating into the past and resonating into the future. It can unearth pain and tenderness (break-ups), softness and joy.

I have loved dancing for as long as I can remember and I have never *not* enjoyed a night out, or a lunch out that turns into a night that turns into a day. The stamina I had was second to none. At seventeen, my friend Lauren and I used to put on skin-coloured stockings, denim miniskirts and tank tops and trek into the city in the middle of winter. We would go to our favourite club on Oxford Street and dance for seven hours straight. I remember sometimes leaving there as the sun was coming up, having sweated so much it was like I had just stepped out of the shower. When I lived in England in my twenties I would go out almost every single night of the week. I travelled all around Europe and partied in Ibiza—I was like a thoroughbred horse that could never be put down. If there was a dance floor, I was on it. I don't want to say I am normally the life of the party because it's totally self-proclaimed but I FUCKEN LOVE A PARTY AND I'M USUALLY THE LIFE OF IT. (*Stay humble, Amz.*) My speciality is weddings. Is there anything better than the union of two wonderful people, celebrating love with good food and a dance floor and everybody dressed to the nines? Weddings are quite possibly my favourite thing in the world, so if you're reading this book and you need a dance-floor starter at your wedding, I AM YOUR WOMAN!

My love for socialising and being out and about with friends was intense in my teens and twenties, and it stemmed from watching my mum and dad be social butterflies. They were never not out with friends or having dinner parties. For their fortieth, fiftieth and sixtieth birthday parties, they threw huge house parties that were always themed. The choice in music was a little different to the stuff I like to dance to but they have always seemed happiest surrounded by their friends and family. Life seemed to consistently flow for them—they were there for us as parents, and they were living their best lives at the same time. Nothing really changed, right? You *can* have both.

My daughter Charli was conceived after a night out when we were most certainly not trying for a baby! We had been at the races and somehow ended up at the Stables, which is a private members area that we somehow got into with friends, and there was a dance floor. Rhian also loves a dance (thank god, otherwise I would have had to end things with him) and one thing led to another. I'm almost certain we were doing the Nutbush one minute and then the next he was pulling out too late. And yes, that is how Charli was conceived.

But motherhood hit me like a freight train and within twelve hours of Charli being born I knew that I was going to be hanging up the dancing shoes momentarily while I tried to get a grip on my new reality. I'm not sure if it's because I really did some living in my twenties, or because I felt like I had been split in half during the birth and couldn't even fathom dropping it low on a dance floor, but life slowed right down for me and I felt more than okay with it. It's the beauty and the curse of having a newborn. Especially your first. It forces you to slow right down, but then there's not a lot to do once you do—apart from heal, if you are anything like me.

My weekends consisted of trying to sleep during the day, or walking the baby to the park and then sitting there watching loads of athletic people running past us. Rhian and I felt like zombies for the first six months of parenting and every part of our relationship changed. Our dynamic and the foundation upon which our relationship had formed—socialising, travelling, being out and about—all kind of stopped. Eating and drinking and dancing were things of the past. Almost as soon as we had started creating a life together, just the two of us . . . *boom*. Now there were three.

The truth was that I kind of really enjoyed the pace of this new life. I enjoyed not waking up with a hangover on Sundays. I loved that our weekends were spent doing things as a family, and it made me look at things with a different perspective. Family was everything to me, and now we had started our own. *This* was what it was all about. Plus I also felt an intense amount of guilt if I even *thought* about leaving Charli. So I didn't. I put myself and my needs well and truly behind hers because I wanted to be everything and more for her. Things really had completely changed for me!

For the first six months of her life, I didn't really do much other than be there for her. I said no to a lot of things because I felt like leaving her was the wrong thing to do. I wish someone had told me that it's perfectly fine to duck out for a quick meal with a girlfriend here and there! I got so caught up in the bizarre mentality of thinking that putting my needs before hers wasn't the right thing to do, and I eventually ended up burning myself out.

When I was twenty-one and working in one of my first media jobs, there was a PA called Katrina. One Monday, I mentioned that I had seen her down at the local bar over the weekend. I also mentioned that she and her friends had all looked totally wasted— they were falling off chairs and accidentally slipping over on the dance floor. She looked at me and said, 'That's because we are mums and we don't get to go out as often anymore. So when we do, we really make up for lost time.' I looked at her blankly, thinking, *Why would having kids change your lifestyle habits? How ridiculous!*—like the naive, childless rookie that I was. As I walked away, she added, 'The more kids you have, the wilder you go', and then winked at me because she had recently had her third.

When Charli was about six months old, we began lubing ourselves up to head back out into the socialising world. It was mainly for bigger-picture type stuff, like weddings and engagement parties. I remember the very first time I left Charli with my mum was when she was only three months old. It was for my own thirtieth birthday and I lasted only three hours. I had gone to an outdoor pub called the Golden Sheaf in Double Bay to have dinner and a glass of wine with some friends, having pumped multiple bottles of milk for Mum to give Charli. The night was filled with all my favourite people, and I tried to enjoy myself while spending the majority of it in the toilet, leaning over the handwashing basin and milking myself like a dairy cow. I couldn't wait to get home to Charli and to throw her immediately onto the tit to relieve myself of the pressure. It definitely wasn't the thirtieth I had planned in my head only a year before!

Fast-forward another three years and our little unit of three had become five. Slowly but surely I had absolutely found my rhythm as a mum and Rhian had been excelling in his role as dad. We were both doing (in my humble opinion) a pretty good job at parenting and we both started to enjoy going out a little bit more. Our speciality was weddings and as parents of three you could really pick us out from the crowd. We don't really have a middle gear. We are either drinking or we are driving, and if you invite us to your wedding Rhian will remove his shirt at some point, I'll get everyone up doing the Nutbush and there will be limited water consumed.

Having a good support network is what makes all the difference. Knowing that your children are safe and being cared for means you can really let your hair down and enjoy yourself! If you don't have in-laws or family close by, invest and get to know some wonderful babysitters. Talk to the educators at preschool, get recommendations from friends. Now that my parents aren't close by anymore we have about three babysitters on rotation and my kids get beyond excited to see them when they turn up. Plus I trust them implicitly and can always relax and breathe easy when they are babysitting.

I wish First-Time Mum Amy had been told how crucial it is to take some time out of parenting. A rite of passage after you've had children should be to organise a girls' night out—whether it's with your old school friends, your new friends, your mum friends or the girl you met in the women's toilets after a few too many wines back in the day.

No one, and I mean *no one*, is more deserving of a girls' night out and a good time than a mum. She needs some time to just feel like herself again. It doesn't necessarily have to involve alcohol and a dance floor (although, when these two things are combined, it can result in a sensational night out, speaking from experience!). It might be a nice vegan dinner followed by some palm reading, a hotel room, a cheese platter, a face mask and a sleep-in.

Whatever it is that your heart desires, make sure you are consistently making time for yourself. A happy, recharged mum is a way more patient mum, after all. All you really have to do is outline a few key things to ensure that whoever is looking after your kids has it covered. You want to set them up for success, because success means they'll nail it and leave you the fuck alone to enjoy your night.

I remember one of the first nights I had organised a staycay with my girlfriends, and was leaving Rhian at home for the first time with all three kids. Although he has always been a great hands-on dad, he works long hours and doesn't get home until after they are in bed during the week. Then he was used to having me with him on weekends and I knew the kids inside out. Schedules. Nap times. Food aversions. You name it, I was always the first port of call. So, for his first night alone with all three, I wrote something of a cheat sheet to help him.

It included very casual things, along the lines of:

- Keep air-con on at twenty-three degrees.

- Keep Bobby from streaking outside.

- Kobe will eat dinner at 4.30 p.m. He will want twice the amount I've left behind for him so be prepared to crack open some pouches and don't be alarmed when he shrieks like a dying goat at you. He'll let you know when he's full by going quiet and defecating in his nappy, which will end up behind his ears because of the sitting position.

- Do not let Bobby and Charli help you change Kobe. They mean well but everyone will end up with poo on their fingers, which will then end up on the wall or in Bobby's eye.

- Charli and Bobby eat dinner at 5 p.m. Charli likes to be fed like a baby bird. Bobby will be doing laps of the lounge room with no pants on. Don't be offended if he doesn't acknowledge your orders to sit down [we are still working on his listening skills].

- They only get dessert if they *both* finish dinner. Keep an eye on Charli because she will excuse herself to use the loo multiple times. Spoiler alert: she's spitting mouthfuls into the bin. [Our kids will literally do anything for dessert.]

- Don't take your eyes off Kobe. When he's not hovering next to the table trying to finger his siblings' bowls, he is a Dyson on legs and will suck every single crumb off the floor.

- MAKE SURE YOU GIVE THEM BOTH THE SAME COLOUR ICE CREAM OR THERE WILL BE WAR.

- Run the bath at 5.45 p.m., get the water to 42.5 degrees. Belly-button height. Everyone gets a bath bomb (except Kobe). Try to stop Bobby from eating his.

- Put all three on the toilet before the bath otherwise they will *all* piss in the bath and you will end up with it splashed all over your face.
- Charli will pick her own pyjamas. This can take up to twenty-eight attempts. DO NOT INTERFERE WITH THIS PROCESS. Attempt to get 'crinkles' out of her pants.
- Bobby will make you chase him around the house forty-three times as he nude-air-dries himself, and dressing him is like dressing a pitbull puppy.
- Kobe will begin malfunctioning around 6 p.m. Bottle is in the fridge on the top shelf. Heat it up for forty-five seconds. Put a bib on him and a bath sheet on you because he's the Vomatron 1000. Feed him on a seventy-eight-degree angle in your arms. Be ready for the burp.
- Kobe goes to bed at 6.15 p.m. Put him in a cocoon; ensure white noise is so loud it sounds like a Russian fighter jet to block out Charli and Bobby. Lay him in his cot and walk out.
- Read Charli and Bobby two books. They get to choose one each. Charli will choose *Cinderella* because it's the longest book in the bookcase. Do not attempt to skip pages or lines because she has memorised every single word. Bobby will do whatever Charli says and will pick the second-longest book there is. Which she has also memorised. This can sometimes take up to thirty minutes.
- Charli and Bobby bed: 7 p.m.
- Charli will want water.
- Charli will want face tickles.

- Charli will want you to lie next to her.
- Spend the next hour putting Bobby back to bed multiple times.
- And lastly, DO NOT CALL ME. By the time you get to this point, I will have had too many wines and be deeply invested in my small breather of freedom, so keep going.
- You're doing great, sweetie!

Pretty sure it's the first and last list I ever wrote for him. I'm not sure if I was even trying to be helpful or using it more as a not-so-subtle 'Look At Everything I Do' list to show him the continuous mental ticker tape of never-ending things there are to do for the kids.

And I don't know about anyone else reading this book, but the first couple of nights I went out after having three kids were pretty tame. What I realised was that going out and giving it a slight nudge, then waking up to not one or two but three children was some sort of fresh hell. Kids don't care that you've gone out the night before. They want to play. They want toast at 5.30 a.m. They want to shit their pants and tell you about it from downstairs while you want to lay in bed upstairs and nurse your poorly head. The thing that really changes dramatically after having kids is how brutal the hangovers are, and how much longer it takes you to bounce back from a big night out.

So while life definitely does change pace there for a while, and all the things you loved doing fade away into the background momen-tarily, you *will* find yourself again. If it's socialising that you love, you will get back out there to those girls' lunches or that dance floor. You might be the oldest one on it, and the twenty-one-year-olds might look at you like you're Stifler's Mom on the sauce, but you will honestly not care, because the days and nights out are what help you keep sane. They help fill up your cup. No one really knows how to let their hair down better than a mum who has been put through the ringer all day long.

Whatever it is that makes you feel alive, *do more of that*. Just make sure you've fed the kids, dropped them off at your parents' or in-laws', and put a Hydralyte and two Nurofen next to your bed.

Now go feel like your young and carefree self again (just with weaker knees and slight incontinence issues)!

ULTIMATE GIRLS' NIGHT OUT PLAYLIST TO GET THOSE HIPS MOVING

Curated by yours truly.

- 'Pony'—Ginuwine (I mean, you knew this was coming)
- 'Murder on the Dancefloor'—Sophie Ellis-Bextor
- 'E.I.'—Nelly
- 'The Brick Track Versus Gitty Up'—Salt-N-Pepa
- 'No Scrubs'—TLC
- 'No Diggity'—Blackstreet ft. Dr. Dre and Queen Pen
- 'Fantasy'—Mariah Carey ft. Ol' Dirty Bastard
- 'My Humps'—Black Eyed Peas
- 'I'm Real (Murder Remix)'—Jennifer Lopez ft. Ja Rule
- 'Big Energy'—Latto
- 'Family Affair'—Mary J. Blige
- 'Gimme More'—Britney Spears
- 'One, Two Step'—Ciara ft. Missy Elliott
- 'Just Dance'—Lady Gaga ft. Colby O'Donis
- 'Say My Name'—Destiny's Child
- 'Ride'—Ciara ft. Ludacris
- 'Hypnotize'—The Notorious B.I.G.
- 'Only You'—112 ft. The Notorious B.I.G. and Ma$e
- 'Too Close'—Next
- 'This is How We Do it'—Montell Jordan
- 'Push It'—Salt-N-Pepa
- 'Forever'—Chris Brown
- 'Gold Digger'—Kanye West ft. Jamie Foxx

- 'Let Me Blow Ya Mind'—Eve ft. Gwen Stefani
- 'Goodies'—Ciara ft. Petey Pablo
- 'Get Right'—Jennifer Lopez
- 'Who's That Girl?'—Eve
- 'Gangsta's Paradise'—Coolio ft. L.V.
- 'Buy U a Drank (Shawty Snappin')'—T-Pain
- 'Always on Time'—Ja Rule ft. Ashanti
- 'Dance With Me'—112
- 'I'm Sprung'—T-Pain
- 'Love in this Club'—Usher ft. Jeezy
- 'Me & U'—Cassie
- 'Tell Me'—Groove Theory
- 'You Make Me Wanna'—Usher
- 'Dilemma'—Nelly ft. Kelly Rowland

SELF-ESTEEM AND SELF-CONFIDENCE

Expectation: It doesn't matter what you look like, it's what's inside that counts

Reality: Confident until I wasn't, became a walking skid mark, then motherhood changed everything

Growing up with two brothers, plus a mum who was—and still is—very much a tomboy, I was the least girly of girls. I don't remember ever having Barbies or having coffee dates with my mum. I don't remember ever dressing up in her heels, because she never wore any. I'd never really break into her make-up drawer either, because I would only ever see her wearing make-up once every solar eclipse. She never even went to the hairdresser. While my next-door neighbour's mum wore dresses, mine wore my dad's baggy t-shirts to mow the lawn. She loved being outdoors and being active. She never really stopped around the house, either, always washing or doing the gardening. She was a total natural beauty, and a leggy one at that. At one point in her life she had been a runway model, which I'm totally not surprised about because her legs go on forever (these did not get passed down to me, unfortunately).

On the odd occasion when my parents went out for a birthday celebration or a dinner party without us kids tagging along, I would sit on Mum's bed and watch her get ready. She had a small collection of earrings and she would always hold two different pairs up to her ears and let me pick which ones she'd wear. Her skincare routine was non-existent and I'm pretty sure she has never even owned a bottle of foundation. She would very lightly dust a bit of blush on the apples of her cheeks and pick a lipstick colour that was neither red nor brown but somewhere in the middle. For as long as I can remember she would always spray a bit of Anais Anais on her wrists and on her neck, comb her hair back and that would be it. I thought she always looked perfect.

Mum always tried to teach me that beauty is on the inside and that what you look like doesn't really bear any resemblance to who you are underneath your skin—that none of it matters as long as you are a good person who thinks of others often. She said it was always better to be natural, so that when you did put some make-up on everyone would be blown away—as opposed to always walking round with make-up on and no one really knowing what you looked like naturally. Through my younger years I believed every single word that left her mouth, but around the age of ten I started to realise that I was in fact quite different-looking to a lot of the other kids at my school. Where their skin would often be sun-kissed all year round, I was deathly white. Of British descent, I was definitely more English rose—of the 'hold the rose and just add a bit of anaemic paleness' variety. Where all of my friends had straight hair, I had super-tight-ringlet curly hair and I didn't know anyone else whose hair was the same colour as mine. It was a strawberry blonde that would throw a lot of red in the sunshine but would always be littered with natural blonde streaks in the middle of summer. My mum used to do this insane thing where she would brush my curls and I would walk around looking like I had been caught jabbing forks into power points. A real looker.

The thing that seemed to make me look the most different from all my friends at school was my freckles. Some of my girlfriends had a light spattering of freckles across their nose but I had them everywhere: all over my face, and down my arms and my legs. Everyone knows that when you have freckles, if you go out in the sun they come out even more, and because we were a family that spent most of our free time and weekends outdoors you can imagine how many freckles I had by the end of every summer. I also did Nippers (junior lifesaving), so I spent a lot of time on the beach and would come home with a raging freckle-face.

By the age of twelve, I hated them. I obsessed bitterly over my appearance, which seems so shallow and vain in hindsight but most of us don't have a whole lot else going on in our lives at that age, apart from school. So cute clothes and *Dolly* magazines were highlights.

A few incidents in my teens changed my self-esteem path, and I remember them distinctly. Having grown up in a family that never prioritised beauty or appearance, I didn't really know what I was walking into when I went to a girls' sleepover in Year 7. I turned up in pedal pushers and a t-shirt, with my hair slicked back into a ponytail. Truth be told, I looked a little bit like a boy but who cared? I was there for the party, and my looks didn't matter. Right? When I got there and looked around the room, I realised I had not read the brief. (There wasn't a brief, but if there had been one it would have read: 'Pretty dresses, braided hair, eyeshadow and lipstick.) And there I was, looking like I was about to head to the skate park.

We got on with the party and ended up playing truth or dare. I was sitting next to a girl who I thought was my friend, and someone asked her 'truth or dare'. She said dare and someone dared her to: 'Tell Amy what you said about her at netball training.' Everyone laughed and I felt like my heart had dropped into my stomach. This felt different from all the times my brothers had given me shit. Turned out my so-called friend had said something along the lines of: 'Amy would be so pretty if she wasn't covered in so many ugly freckles.' I remember just laughing it off and throwing back some silly insult about her not being a great goal shooter, and then I went and sat on the toilet and cried. It seems so ridiculous now, as I type this out as a grown-ass thirty-seven-year-old, but we all know how big those little feelings are at age thirteen. I felt totally humiliated—and angry at Mum and Dad for giving me such awful skin.

Fast-forward to Year 10 and I had become a bit of a tomboy myself. Never wore make-up, rarely wore anything girly, was pretty good at sport and played a lot of it—though I always *loved* dancing. I wasn't really paid much attention by guys for the first couple of years of high school because I'm almost certain they were trying to work out whether I was male or female. But I was pretty loud and boisterous, and I adapted pretty quickly to having insults thrown at me because of my appearance. I worked out real quick that if I could be self-deprecating first, their words couldn't hurt me.

So I was always the first to take the piss out of myself. I called myself 'The Ranga' before anyone else could. Any insult I thought was coming my way I'd use on myself first. It was a weird and negative headspace to be in, but it was also the way I protected myself.

A guy from my year asked me to go to Year 10 formal with him, just as friends, but even then I got so awkward that I wrestled him to the ground—and accidentally punched him in the mouth and made his lip bleed. I was stoked—it was a yes from me. I went in a metallic-blue strapless dress and my mum curled my hair for me. She stuck little diamantes all through the curls, too, and I wore a tiny little bit of mascara and lip gloss. I looked like Snow White in a metallic dress but if you ask my parents, they'll say I was the most beautiful girl there. The formal was so much fun and afterwards we all went home to get changed and then go to the afterparty.

It was a house party at the house of one of the guys in my year, and it was just around the corner from where we lived so Mum dropped me and some girlfriends off and said she would pick us up at 11 p.m. My friends and I had been talking about what we were going to wear to the afterparty for at least ten months and I had settled on a denim skirt and a white singlet top. Iconic, I know.

I remember sitting outside in the cul-de-sac, drinking a raspberry UDL, when all these boys from a different school rocked up and started talking to us. We sat outside for a good hour chatting with them, and there was one guy in particular who I was getting along with really well. His mates were giving him shit about having a crush on me, and you couldn't tell because we were sitting in the dark but I was blushing from head to toe. I felt like I had a crush on him too. When it started to get a bit cold, we all began to move inside to get more drinks and when we did so, I was standing next to said boy when all his mates started screaming: 'No fucken way, bro, look at her! She's covered in freckles! They are even on her legs—that's so gross!'

I stood frozen to the spot and thought I might be sick. Everyone had turned around to stare at me and I so badly wanted the ground to open up and swallow me. I could tell the guy I had been talking to was torn. He didn't seem to care that I had freckles but from the way his mates were carrying on he obviously felt like he had no choice but to leave me standing there and walk away. Some were calling me 'Cheetah' and others were asking if they could play connect the dots. I felt so humiliated and so embarrassed that even bringing this memory up makes me want to cry, and it makes me want to run to that sixteen-year-old version of myself and hold onto her. Because I remember how I felt in that very moment. Like I was so unlovable. Not worthy of having a boy who was interested in me. I was made to feel like some sort of hideous beast because of the freckles that I could do absolutely nothing about.

It's a moment that has stayed with me for my whole life. It absolutely crushed any little bit of self-esteem that I'd had left. I went home and spent hours on Yahoo searching how to bleach my skin. What I did was buy foundation—so much foundation—and I didn't only wear it on my face but all over my arms and my legs as well. It was the most ridiculous time of my life and one that I'm sure my parents absolutely struggled with, but I was struggling too: with some HUGE hormone fluctuations, and with self-esteem that was completely bruised and battered. I also had a complete and utter lack of care when it came to bedding and bath towels in my home. Not only that, any time I walked past someone and bumped shoulders with them, I would literally leave a skid mark. I was a walking skid mark. The only times I felt better were when my freckles were covered up.

After that, I quickly turned from an outgoing, sporty tomboy into someone who wore *heavy* make-up daily. When I left school and got my first job, I would apply make-up as if I was going to a wedding every morning. My girlfriend Kacee was the one who initially got me into make-up, and after make-up it was fake tan. *Hurrah!* Finally a product that would help stain the other parts of my skin that weren't freckled and would blend everything all together! Add foundation over the top and I had everyone convinced for years that I was actually of Mediterranean descent. I know as you are reading this you are probably thinking I looked like an Oompa Loompa straight out of the Willy Wonka factory, but I promise I actually did a not-too-bad job of making sure my excessive faux skin colour wasn't too shonky-looking.

You see, the thing is, when I thought I looked better I *felt* better. I was adamant that I was going to transform into something that guys liked the look of. When my self-esteem was up, so was my confidence. I put a lot of effort into making sure guys liked me— liked the look of me. I craved attention and wanted to feel wanted. Thirty-seven-year-old Amy wants to go back in time and bitch-slap herself, but after the rejection and devaluing I felt all through high school, I thought the only route to getting over feeling like that was to change the way I looked, so that men would deem me acceptable to date or ask out.

For almost a decade, from my early teens to early twenties, my insecurity was masked by vanity and a need to always look good. I put *so* much emphasis on how I looked. You couldn't pay me to go to the beach, swimming, around boys. NEVER. I still lived an incredible life, but at my core I was nervous about the way I looked. All of my mum and dad's hard work trying to make me understand that being beautiful is about so much more than what you look like seemed to just be a distant memory, but I truly believed that an uncompromised version of self-confidence was something that you were simply born with. If you looked like Adriana Lima. If you were what society deemed beautiful.

As an eighteen-year-old, I truly thought that in order to be loved or worthy you had to be physically beautiful, and therefore I assumed my obsession with camouflaging my freckles and dyeing my hair was something that I would have forever.

My mum did more than enough for me as I was growing up. She was constantly trying to change the way I thought of myself. She was always trying to instil a sense of self-worth in me, but her words fell on deaf ears for a while. Her voice was etched into my heart; it just got buried for so many years under pain and hurt from cruel kids. But eventually all the core values and lessons she taught me came back to the surface.

She had always told me I was beautiful, but mostly when I was thinking of others or doing something kind for someone else, or when I showed independence or was brave in the face of adversity. She also said it when I was coming off a netball court covered in sweat, or dirty and messy and working hard. Mum and Dad always said that beauty lies within you, in the way you make others feel and the kindness you put out into the world, not in how you look.

Confidence in who you are as a person is definitely not a switch that you can flick on overnight. It's a long, uphill battle to find yourself, and to find out that all the things you once thought were so important aren't, in fact. Like how the silly kids used to give you shit about your freckles. Or how the boys in your street would push you over because you had red hair and they said rangas were gross. Or how Greg Hannah called you 'Train Tracks' when you got your braces on in Year 9 and refused to sit next to you on the bus. Or how your first boyfriend stopped you from eating dessert with him because your thighs touched and you didn't have a thigh gap. What I would do to go back in time and give those wombats a left hook! But, to be honest, they would probably be mortified with themselves too.

I never thought I would get to the place I am now with it. Only with time and life experiences do you start to realise that all of these little things, and people's opinions of you, don't matter. Only then do you realise that not giving a fuck is one of the greatest skills in life you can learn.

Not giving a fuck sounds like apathy, but I promise you it's not. It doesn't make you an asshole or mean you are selfish. It means you are looking out for yourself. It puts you in a healthier headspace and will make you a better person to be around. It will free you enormously from the inhibitions that society has given you, or that you have given yourself. Not giving a fuck is simply a refusal to waste your energy and time on negative thoughts, and it took me almost thirty years to finally get here.

Having said that, there are so many things in life that we *do* need to care about. Our own happiness is obviously the number-one priority, and there are also the friends and family members we care about, looking after our bodies and working on whatever aspirations we have. Yet there is also an overwhelming amount of shit that we spend hours, days and even months obsessing over that never really matters. For so many years, I gave too many fucks about what people thought of me and my appearance, and I lived my life enslaved to those opinions. Those thoughts would fill up my head and distance me from the life that was still unfolding in front of me. It was completely self-destructive.

I was so busy giving a fuck about all the things around me that I had practically stopped living. The more desperately I wanted to be like someone else, the more unworthy I felt. The more desperately I wanted to feel happier, the lonelier I became. The more I tried to live up to the expectations of others—to be what, and who, others deemed beautiful and attractive—the more miserable I felt.

Everything really changed for me when I moved to the UK. I was twenty-one and I was on my own, with nothing but a few email chains linking me to my mum and dad. I lived and travelled and grew as a person, working in London and then taking off for six weeks every year to see as much of Europe as I possibly could. There I was, on the other side of the world, travelling to Croatia, swimming in the Ionian Sea, dancing on tables in Greece. *This is what life was meant to be all about*, I thought. *This is what my mum always used to talk about. This is why she always told me not to worry about my looks.*

It was then that I really focused on the art of not giving a fuck and just living life. I simply stopped caring about the opinions of those who didn't matter to me.

In London, I was working in a little pub in Clapham South called Gigalum. I would work in advertising during the day, and at the pub at night-time and on the weekends. I also lived upstairs (that was a wild time in my life). I remember one of my very first shifts there. I was serving an English guy who I had seen a few times. He ended up sitting at the bar and we chatted for most of the afternoon. There was no romantic interest there—he was just so lovely to talk to. I finished my shift and sat down for a cider with him, telling him all about Australia and what Sydney was like. He stopped me halfway through a sentence and told me that he thought my freckles were the most gorgeous thing he'd ever seen, and that they reminded him of his mum. He said that staring at a woman's face that had no freckles was like looking at a night sky without stars. It's still one of the sweetest things anyone has ever said to me. And no, I did not sleep with him afterwards (although I thought about it).

By that stage I was already in a much better headspace. I knew that, looks aside, I was a real hoot to be around. But it was just so interesting to see how people can have such different perspectives on things.

When I stopped caring about nonsense and things I couldn't control, I started caring more about the things that really *did* matter.

My family. My friends. The opportunities I had. The travel, which seemed endless. I realised that I had more time and energy to dedicate to the things, and people, that I did love and that made me happy. Living life to the fullest comes from knowing what to care about and, most importantly, what not to care about. I don't really know if there was a trigger to all this, or if it really was just a slow burn over time. But I knew I was tired of trying to appease others. I started to believe in myself and what I could offer the world. I knew my self-worth.

By the time I was in my late twenties, I felt confident in who I was as a person, and in what I could offer in all different types of relationships, whether platonic or romantic. I did not put up with anyone's bullshit. I was never going to let anyone drag me or my self-esteem down again.

Then, when I had my first child, well . . . *shit*. Afterwards I felt like a goddamn warrior. Motherhood does something incredibly special to a woman's self-confidence, give or take the first couple of months when you feel like roadkill—but even when I looked like Charlize Theron in *Monster* I still felt invincible. My body was battered and bruised and full of little scars, like a map of the journey I had been on, but I was so proud of it. In my early twenties I was covered head to toe in foundation, hair always ironed straight and make-up on daily, and I was always fixated on maintaining a certain weight. After my first kid, I barely washed my hair, would occasionally wear make-up on the weekends if I had something on, my left tit weighed about 55 kilos, my legs hadn't seen the sun in months and were a light shade of purple they were that pale, my thighs chafed just walking to the coffee shop, my face was spotty and white in between all the kisses from the sun that would be on show after a shower . . . and yet I was the most confident I had ever been in my life. Because I knew I was SO MUCH MORE THAN HOW I LOOK. I was a motherfucken human-life creator/grower/birther/titty-feeder/keeper-aliver. I created a human and here I was keeping it alive with my body. My once half-empty confidence cup was overflowing because I was responsible for something so much more important than my looks. I have been fearlessly accepting myself ever since becoming a mum, and consequently hope my children master the art of self-love (and hopefully in less time than it took me to!).

Motherhood helped me to finally come into my own and become the person I always felt like I should have been, or that I always wanted to be. I feel more grounded, free and comfortable in my own skin than I ever have before. Self-confidence is not a gift that is engraved into your DNA. It's also not something that you get from others when they pat you on the back. Self-confidence comes from small victories and successes. It's those baby steps and trial-and-error situations that will help your confidence flourish, allowing you to tackle even bigger challenges. In my case, one of those bigger challenges was having three kids . . . my first two were the trial-and-error babies, lol.

Today I truly have such little time or care for what other people think of me that I live completely and utterly without inhibitions.

This morning I went to grab a coffee, fresh-faced in Rhian's oversized t-shirt, and it was only when I was walking into the coffee shop that I realised I had forgotten to wear pants. Twenty-one-year-old Amy would have NEVER. When I think of who I am as a person and how I'm perceived, my physical appearance doesn't even come into it. I still have freckles (although faded dramatically now). I am kind, thoughtful and considerate, and would give the shirt off my back to anyone who needed it. I bring a good energy and will always strive to make you laugh. My friendship door is always open, and I love listening to people and helping where I can.

I'm definitely not everyone's cup of tea but who would want to be? I know who I am and what I have to offer. My focus in life is to be happy, and my motto of not giving a fuck is not about being rude: it is simply about refusing to focus on negative energy. If I could go back in time to my sweet sixteen-year-old self and tell her that beauty is just a superficial quality that does not reflect the true essence of a person's character, values or personality, I would—but I doubt she would listen. Our looks can be deceiving, as they really don't have any correlation to our depth, kindness and intelligence as individuals. No one should *ever* define someone solely based on their appearance, but rather on their actions, beliefs and inner qualities.

Finding self-confidence, and learning to love and accept yourself, is an ongoing process that takes time and effort, but it can definitely be achieved by focusing on a few key areas.

Here are my tips on how you can be kinder to yourself.

1. Identify your strengths—the things you are good at. Are you a good listener? Do you have a great energy that people want

to be around? Do you make people feel included? Are you an exceptional cook who loves feeding people? List your positive qualities, achievements and skills. Then make sure you always celebrate your successes and acknowledge your abilities. Bring those to the forefront when you meet new people and be proud of what kind of person you are by sharing these parts of yourself with others.

2. Challenge your negative thoughts. When you look at yourself in the mirror, I want you to say out loud three things that you love about your appearance. For example: 'I love the way my eyes smile when I smile.' Recognise your negative self-talk and challenge it with positive affirmations. Treat yourself with kindness and compassion, and be gentle when you make mistakes or experience setbacks. Replace negative thoughts with positive ones, and focus again on your strengths and all that you have accomplished. (I'm not just talking about negative thoughts about your appearance here; it might be your career, or your role as a mother, or anything.) Your brain is so powerful and *you* have control over it. Sometimes when I lie in bed at night after watching the news, my thoughts can turn to all the horrible things that could potentially happen to my kids. So I sit up in bed and I tell myself that they are safe and loved, and then I try to picture them at their twenty-first birthday parties or at their weddings. (I'm still unsure if this is something I need to go and actually talk to a counsellor about, or if it's just normal worried-mum stuff, but I digress . . .)

3. Practise self-care. Take care of your physical and emotional well-being by trying to get enough sleep ('trying' being the operative

word when you are a mum), eating a healthy diet (with Oporto occasionally) and exercising two or three times a week (can also just be chasing after kids, because that's what I did heavily for four years: I was a platinum member at my own home gym). Do things that genuinely make your heart soar! Go out dancing with your girlfriends. Buy yourself a new dress for a nice lunch with your mum. Book yourself an international trip. Get yourself a killer blow-dry and go out for a nice meal with your partner. When you feel good about yourself, you are more likely to feel confident!

4. Learn to say no to things, and 'Piss off' to people who make you sad and situations that don't serve you well. Set boundaries and set them firmly, to protect your time and your energy.

5. Step out of your comfort zone when you can. The best thing I ever did was book a one-way flight to England. It changed everything for me and proved to me that I was capable of handling new situations and challenges. It pushes you to step up in areas that you wouldn't normally step up in. It's scary but so, *so* rewarding, and will help your confidence flourish at the same time.

6. Focus on what *does* make you feel good. Invest in some nice skincare and a few pieces of make-up to accentuate your natural beauty. Book yourself in for a haircut or change up your colour. Try something new to mix things up. Change is always good, especially if you feel like you are in a bit of a rut. Buy yourself a new outfit that complements your shape. (None of this needs to be expensive.) Flirt with a cute barista, go dancing with your girlfriends and let your hair down, and *never* compare yourself to

women online. Remember that the only person's opinion of how you look (that matters) is *yours*, so invest the time in falling back in love with yourself!

7. Surround yourself with positive people who support and encourage you in all facets of your life. You are the company you hang around so choose your tribe wisely. And stay the fuck out of toxic relationships.

8. My final tip—and some of you will probably roll your eyes when you read this—is GRATITUDE. Focusing on what you have rather than what you lack instantly changes your entire mindset. There's always good stuff going on in your life, even on the darkest days when you feel like you are drowning in the bad. Without trying to sound like a walking motivational quote/tosser, I think that if you shift your mindset to a positive one, your perspective towards things will change over time too. I practise gratitude daily. And in turn I've made positive thinking a habit. I look for the silver linings in the everyday. I laugh off the things I can't control and work on the things I can. I try every day to be a better person and a better mum for my kids, and every time I screw up along the way (read: all the time), I get back up and try again. You can practise gratitude for anything from watching the sun rise to the delicious brekkie you made without setting anything on fire, feeling safe in your neighbourhood, hitting climax multiple times before your partner does, or even booking a girls' trip. All of these things are wonderful things to be grateful for. Never compare yourself. Think of others frequently. Try not to be an asshole.

BIRTH

Expectation: Just like doing the biggest poo of your life

Reality: Delivering a baby and a poo simultaneously while feeling 4600 bones in your body are being crushed

As I have already mentioned, the expectations I had for birthing my babies were pretty optimistic. The only intel I was ever fed was from my mum, who absolutely LOVED being pregnant and always described giving birth nonchalantly, in a 'no biggie' kind of way. The more I write in this book, the more I realise that so many of my life expectations were centred around her past experiences and the way she would relay them to me. Never mind the fact that your body literally produces a drug in your brain so that you forget certain experiences, e.g. CHILDBIRTH. Now I think about it, I don't remember her ever going into many details. She left a lot of the gory stuff out, either by choice or because as you age you truly *do* remember things with rose-coloured glasses on.

I was always curious about things relating to pregnancy and birth and if you had asked me what I wanted to be in life my first answer was always 'a mum'. Childbirth was the final step to getting there and it sounded like a minor hurdle. Mum had three kids: two vaginally and one out the sunroof. There was never much talk of pain or epidurals. All Mum ever had was gas. I assumed all I would ever have would be gas. I wanted to be just like her when I grew up. She paved the way for me in so many things, in ways I'm sure she wasn't even aware of.

Some women like to try to picture how they think labour will go and how they will handle the situation. The more prep they do, the more educated they are on the process, and the more seamless they expect things to be. I used to try to picture myself giving birth because I'd heard it was a helpful way to prepare for the intensity of childbirth. A midwife once said that when we start to worry about birthing, there's something within us that automatically starts looking for solutions. It activates our brains to start thinking of resources, both inner and outer, and bring out the part of us, as women, that does in fact know what to do.

I did not do this. I am a fly-by-the-seat-of-my-pants kinda gal, a true winger of life. I did go and do three calm-birthing classes, which were all about breathing and how important it was to focus on that. Breathe in for four and out for four. Got it. I went into my first labour being very casual and almost a little bit overconfident . . . and was *so* goddamn unprepared.

At 4 a.m. on 23 December 2015, having come home from a midwife appointment the day before at thirty-six weeks and six days and saying that I was *sure* this baby was coming at thirty-seven weeks, my waters broke. I'm not sure if I had been low-key manifesting that because it hurt to exist, or if the excess fluid in my uterus had just hit capacity and it busted out like a water balloon hitting hot tarmac. I remember going to the toilet for the eighty-seventh time that night and, as I walked back to bed, I could feel liquid dripping out of me. *Oh god, I've now hit the pelvic incontinence stage*, I thought, but the liquid kept coming. I woke Rhian up and by 5 a.m. I had soaked through multiple towels and could have filled up a small kids' paddling pool (okay, I'm exaggerating). *Holy shit*, I realised, *my waters have broken—this is it, I'm having a baby today!*

Off we went to the hospital after breakfast. There was no pain or contractions but I thought I must have been at least seven centimetres dilated because I had been doing my deep breaths in and deep breaths out, oh and my waters had broken five hours ago, so *obviously* it would be time to push soon. We turned up with my hospital bag, ready to rock and roll, but they asked to examine me first. The midwife had a little look-see down below and popped her head up between my legs to tell me that I was only two centimetres dilated and I should probably just go home. WAIT, WHAT? *Go home?* I was perplexed. *But I'm about to have a baby!*

She ushered us out, telling me to relax and let labour start at home.

'What do you mean, "start"? Isn't this labour? Aren't I in labour now?'

The midwife gave me a gentle rub on the back, probably thinking, *Dear god, this one is going to be a punish*, but told me kindly, 'Not quite. You'll definitely have a better understanding of when you are in labour. Now, if you head home, I'll send a nurse out to give you acupuncture and that'll get the ball rolling.'

Off we went, feeling a little bit silly and also a lot confused. The nurse arrived an hour later and I had acupuncture in the strangest places: tiny metal needles punctured my skin around my spleen, bladder and large intestine; on my ankle, and in between my thumb and pointer finger. I felt nothing while it was happening but within thirty minutes I started to get a dull, aching, period-type pain. I walked down to get a juice with Rhian because I thought being upright would help, but I was also paranoid about the baby plummeting out so I wore two pairs of undies. Thinking back now to how naive and innocent/a little bit stupid I was with my first labour makes me laugh.

By 6 p.m., things had kicked up a notch. I was kind of groaning and moaning but still at home. Surely I was nine centimetres! By 9 p.m. I was in and out of scalding-hot showers. The pain in my lower back was so intense that when I wasn't in the shower I was on all fours in my room mooing like a dairy cow. By this stage I had started to panic and I called the midwife who was on duty and said my pain level was at an eleven out of ten. She asked if she could listen to how frequently my contractions were coming. After being on the phone to me for a good fifteen minutes she said, 'Take two Panadol and try and get some sleep. Come in first thing in the morning.'

WHAT THE FUCK? You want me to sleep? And pop in tomorrow morning? I feel like it was at this very moment that I spiralled. All the calmness that had been slowly draining out of me dropped to zero and instead of staying focused on the situation at hand, I became wildly panicked. Every bad scenario possible played out in my head. What if I gave birth on the carpet? We would never get the bond back. What if the baby came out not breathing? What if something happened to me? I wished that phone call with the midwife had never happened, because things might have played out differently, but I ended up calling my mum in hysterics: 'THEY WON'T LET ME COME INTO THE HOSPITAL, MUM . . . WAHHHHHH . . . THEY ARE FORCING A HOME BIRTH ON ME AND . . . WAHHHHHH . . . I'VE ALREADY USED UP ALL THE HOT WATER!'

My mum said, 'Don't be ridiculous. Just get in the car right now and you drive to the hospital.' So that's exactly what we did. I remember every single contraction in the car. I could barely stand by the time I got to the hospital and once we barged through the door and got examined I almost punched Rhian in the dick when they told me I was only four centimetres dilated. HOW? I had been two centimetres ten hours before and the pain levels were now so very, very different. But because I was in panic mode, my brain wasn't allowing my body to do what it needed to do. Instead of breathing through the contractions I would tense like I was doing a sit-up. I would curl up in a ball and hold my breath. Basically every single thing I had learned in that calm-birthing class went out the window and at four centimetres I thought I was going to die. *Verrrrrry* dramatic. I was fighting against everything my body was trying to do and the midwives could see it.

I was given gas. Then two shots of morphine—one in each thigh. That did nothing except make the entire room spin and make me feel nauseous like I was in my first trimester again. I was begging for an epidural but a car-crash victim had come in and the anaesthetist was down in surgery. I was screaming at Rhian to go and buy an epidural from another hospital. He looked so bewildered, like a big deer in the headlights. He was trying to help me but there was absolutely nothing he could do to take the pain away so he just had to sit in it. It must be quite a confronting thing for partners, feeling so helpless.

Anyway, I digress. Finally the epidural was underway. It took three nurses just to get the cannula in my hand, which almost took my mind off the contractions for a split second because I'm almost certain I have nerve damage from that moment . . . finally the cannula was in, the epidural was going into the spine. The anaesthetist tapped up my back and assured me that within fifteen to twenty minutes I would be given some relief and shouldn't be able to feel a thing.

Forty-five minutes later I still felt everything. He had missed the sweet spot. The feeling of him ripping the tape off my back to try again will haunt me for life. I don't know if it's because everything was so hypersensitive but it felt like I was being skinned alive. I cried and begged for mercy, thinking *I bet this wasn't how my mum gave birth to me.*

The second time worked a treat and every single little bit of pain that I had felt fifteen minutes prior was gone. I remember a doctor once saying to me, 'You wouldn't have a filling without anaesthetic, so why would you have a baby without one?' and I completely understand his viewpoint because fifteen minutes before I had thought every single bone in my body was being crushed and now . . . I drifted off to sleep. A relaxed sleep. Eyes closed. I slept. For four hours. When I came to I could feel the contractions again. They were nowhere near as severe as they had been but I had decided that

I already had PTSD from five hours before and *where the fuck is that little top-up button?* I pushed it so many times but I swear they had unplugged me from the juice. A midwife came in to check me and said, 'Oh, it's go time, honey, you are fully dilated. We just need you to push this baby out now.' I asked for more epidural juice, but she told me that I would be able to push more efficiently if I could work with the pain and contractions. For fuck's sake! *First they miss my spine, then I get a taste of the good stuff and now they are ripping it from me again! But whatever—let's get this show over with.*

The pushing part I didn't mind. Did it make me realise how truly unfit I was? Yes. Did I burst most of the capillaries in both my eyes? Yes. Was Rhian screaming at me from the sidelines like a football coach? Yes. Did I want to murder Rhian at that exact point in time? Also yes. But we got there, after a total of thirty-two hours. Along with another two litres of fluid, my tiny, sweet girl arrived on Christmas Eve 2015 at 11:58 a.m. weighing in at a dainty 2.8 kilograms. Now what I really want to say is that she got put on my chest and my heart burst open with love and doves were released while the three of us embraced as a new family. But what actually happened was this purple, alien-looking thing covered in what looked like war paint landed on my chest and then started making this gurgled shrieking sound. I was on Planet So Fkn Exhausted (Population: Me) and I could barely hold her. I felt like I was dropping in and out of consciousness as they were stitching me up down there, but the one clear memory I have of those first few minutes after she was born was the feeling of sheer, utter relief. It was over, and I had Charli: my very own daughter.

If you had asked me for guidance heading into labour after my first birth, my advice would have been to drop all your expectations. Don't even bother with a birthing plan. I know some people have had one in place and it's worked out a treat but more often than not it goes tits-up and doesn't play out in the woman's favour. The fewer expectations you have leading up to this momentous occasion in your life, the better. It will be like nothing you have ever experienced or could possibly prepare for. All the books, podcasts, birthing classes and hypnotherapy in the world can't prepare you for birth. Sure, they can equip you with some tools if you stay in your sane mind, but more often than not all the things you think will happen, and the way you think you will handle the situation, will be instantly abandoned once you are in active labour.

But that Amy was just speaking about her own lived experience, and she hadn't loved her first birth. It turns out I was wrong. Fear of the unknown had taken me prisoner in my first birth, and I can say this wholeheartedly since having had three children now: the *more* you prepare yourself, the better you will be.

All three of my labours have been completely different and I love that I am able to compare them all. My second, with Bobby, was by far the best. My first made so much sense in hindsight, and if I had known what I knew later, Charli's birth would have been so much better.

Everything I had learned in my calm-birthing class came into effect when Bobby was on the way. I was getting induced thanks to cholestasis playing havoc with my liver (R.I.P. the soft skin on the bottom of my feet). I had prewarned the midwives not to fuck with me and that the minute I walked into the delivery suite I would want that epidural in my spine. I had a midwife called Karen with me that day. She was older and she gave off that tough-love kind of vibe. I instantly thought we weren't going to get along and I was going to have to fight her for an epidural but she was a straight shooter and told me upfront that if I wanted an epidural right off the bat, I could potentially be in hospital all day and night. Instead, if I had a crack at doing some labouring myself, she said, then as soon as I wanted to tap out she would deliver the spinal crack to me without me having to ask twice. We kind of gave each other this nod, like a metaphorical handshake, me with a little bit of fear and uncertainty in my eyes, and her eyes saying, 'You've *absolutely* got this, darl.'

Rhian had packed himself a smorgasbord of food and down-loaded multiple movies on his iPad, and was settling in for the day. A doctor came in and broke my waters, and Karen wandered in and turned up the oxytocin drip. She told me she would start off with it low and, as my contractions started to progress, she would just monitor me. I could be wrong but I'm almost certain she turned it up to full blast and then just skipped out of the room. I sat up in the bed and all the teachings from the calm-birthing class came flooding in. I also did not feel scared. I knew what was coming. I knew what a contraction felt like and what to expect so I didn't panic.

I felt safe and secure in the hospital so I just concentrated on my breathing. Rhian was trying to talk to me but I was just doing my inhales and my exhales. He came over to stand next to me at the bed and asked how I was feeling but I was in some sort of river-birthing hippie zone. I felt so in control. He started rubbing my leg up and down, and I remember the warm sensation of his hands on my legs (that would have resembled a yeti's) feeling comforting in some bizarre way. I closed my eyes and every time I had a contraction I would just breathe with it. At the peak of the contraction, when it hurt the most, I would exhale and no word of a lie I could feel my baby moving down inside me. Every time I exhaled, I would try to imagine opening up my butthole as I breathed out. When Karen had been giving me one of her tough-love talks before ramping up the drip to full volume, she said to me, 'Every time you exhale with a contraction, try to push your bumhole as deep as you can into the bed—almost like you're blowing a kiss with your asshole.' I don't know what kind of midwifery magic it was, or just the fact that she had been dealing with pregnant women for more than two decades, but that was the most solid piece of advice I had ever been given.

I was absolutely bossing this labour until ... *ohhhh shit, no I'm not ... KAREN ... KARRRRRRRRRREN ... I NEED THE EPIDURAL, OH SHIT I NEED TO PUSH!* Karen walked in slowly and calmly with a 'God I'm good at my job' look on her face and said, 'I'm just going to lay you back to examine you and then we can get you an epidural.' Before she could even get the bed halfway down, I had to poo. Well, that's what it felt like anyway. There was a deep pressure and something going on inside my butthole and whatever it was it wanted out. *Right then and there.* Karen smiled and said softly, 'Your baby is right here waiting to meet you. You just need to push it out.' Six pushes later and I'd given birth. Again. This time in ninety minutes from the time my waters had broken. They placed the second purple alien on me, a son, born on 11 October 2017 at 10.30 a.m. Rhian hadn't even started on his snack pack.

When we started texting family and friends, everyone was so confused: 'Didn't you just arrive?' I felt absolutely incredible. If I didn't also have to give birth to the placenta I would have jumped off the bed and started fist pumping. It was euphoric and like nothing I had ever experienced before. The rush of adrenaline was insane. In that moment I felt like I could give birth to twenty-five more babies if they went like that. I was in awe of my body and my mind—the way the two had worked so seamlessly together and how everything I'd been taught in that calm-birthing class had paid off. And Karen—what a sly dog! This was all because of her believing in me. Her staunch attitude actually gave me confidence. I will remember her face and her no-fucks-given attitude until my memory starts to fail me. I hope every mum gets a Karen as their midwife once in their lives.

My advice after baby number two: stay present, stay focused and stay with your breath. If you are reading this and are about to have a baby, learn from my mistakes with my first. If you've already had a shitty birth, like I did with my first, and want to give me an uppercut reading this paragraph, I will also understand.

The third and final birth is one that I get a bit emotional talking about. It was the birth of that man-baby growing inside me. I was getting induced again, purely because of the size of him and not wanting to be wheelchair-bound if I let him grow any bigger. I was thirty-eight weeks and even though there was nothing wrong with bub, I had expressed my concerns about being torn from here to China and was desperately trying to avoid that (especially because I had two little ones at home who I also needed to care for). Having been induced for Bobby's birth, I knew the process and how it went. I opted for a drug-free birth again based purely on how good my last labour had been. It would be like reading the same book all over again . . . right?

We dropped Charli and Bobby off to my parents' the night before and told the kids that we would be bringing them home a new brother or sister the following day. Then we said our goodbyes and went home for one last sleep—and by 'sleep', I mean 'small clusters of minutes in which I could close my eyes'.

Birth is so wild that not even my detailed recaps can prepare you for it. It will be one of the most intense moments you will ever experience, in which an entire chapter of your life closes and a new one begins. This time, I woke up at 4 a.m., pumping with adrenaline about who the newest member of our family was going to be. Straight into hospital, and I put on the sexy gown almost immediately. Rhian hadn't even parked the car and they had already broken my waters. By the time he got up to the room, things were moving already. I asked if they could hold off turning on the oxytocin drip and I would do some walking (read: star jumps) in the room and hope to kickstart labour naturally. It did not work. They plugged me into the juice and then I was ready to rock and roll.

We had a birth photographer this time. I hadn't had any pics taken of my previous two births, give or take the shots the midwives took where I look utterly defeated (first time) and like I'm on a pinger/so high (second time). Little did I know this third birth would be the first time I shat myself, so I couldn't have chosen a better birth to photograph, really.

It's funny how a woman's body seems to know exactly what position it wants to be in when labour kicks up a notch. With Charli, I had to be put to sleep to let my body open up, and with Bobby, the pushing-my-butthole-as-far-as-I-could-into-the-bed really worked wonders. But with my third birth, I had to stand. Where Rhian drove me bonkers in my first, and basically did nothing in the second, he was the most incredible support partner with my third. I held onto him almost the whole time. My arms were wrapped around his neck and he would lean into me so I could rest my body on him while trying to breathe through a contraction. We were totally in sync without saying any words, and he knew exactly what I needed in those moments. I also pooed on his shoes, so there's that, too.

After labouring for a good two hours, standing up swaying, my pain really kicked in. A midwife came in to check on me and she said I was eight centimetres. It was almost go time but I knew it would get more painful first. The 'transition phase' of labour is the stage where you are almost ready to start pushing. I like to call it HELL ON EARTH but if you are lucky it will progress quickly, and you'll be at full dilation and pushing in no time. If you are an unlucky son of a bitch, like I was this time, you will hit then transition phase and then come to a pause.

I was constantly feeling the urge to bear down—to push—but I just couldn't feel anything happening. What I *could* feel was every single part of my body about to be split in two. I just kept replaying what that doctor had said to me about not having a filling without anaesthetic. Just kidding—there was not a single rational thought crossing my brain at this point. I was acutely aware that something wasn't going to plan but I couldn't work out what it was. I was in a standing-up position trying my hardest to push but the only thing that was coming out was poo, and it was going all over Rhian's feet. I mean, I hadn't pooed during my two first births so the third time was obviously a charm for me. But it was the absolute last thing I cared about.

The room went from having just me, Rhian and our midwife in it to having a second midwife. They were getting me up on the bed on all fours and asking me to hug the bed and try to push that way but it wasn't working. I kept trying to stand back up because for some reason that felt the most natural. The monitors over my belly had started to show that baby was in distress so back onto my back I went and started to actively push and push. At one point I was certain that I was going to pop my own eyeballs out of my head but the adrenaline kept me focused.

Someone pressed something and the room filled with people. A doctor came over to me and I begged her to cut the baby out. I almost couldn't talk at this point through the pain. This was nothing like my other two births. She explained that she wouldn't be able to do that because the baby was already far too engaged and she was going to give me an episiotomy. By then I would have agreed to have my legs removed to end the pain; it was like nothing I can put into words. Sorry if you're about to give birth next week.

The next twenty minutes kind of went by in a blur. I was aware of stuff going on down below but the burning ring of fire was by far the most prominent feeling. I had the doctor in between my legs, two midwives behind her and another five or so people in the room behind them. I could hear the urgency in their voices, telling me to push and to keep going. I was terrified. I also wanted to punch someone in the face every time they told me to push because I was not sitting there knitting.

But every time I felt like I couldn't possibly go on, I was able to tap into some unknown reserve of Xena: Warrior Princess strength. I just *knew* I had to keep going. The head was there and if I could just find it within me to push a few more times I knew I could get it out. What I didn't realise—and I don't think any of the midwives or doctors did, either—was that the umbilical cord had wrapped around my baby's neck multiple times and every time I pushed it was like my baby was being strangled.

When I felt the head pop out I almost fainted. I had two ladies either side of me trying to keep me awake and telling me to just work with the next contraction to get the body out. Our baby was born not breathing and it was the scariest moment of my life. The photographer who had been there with us for the entire process had to put her camera away when they pushed the alarm. But once I got Kobe out, she pulled out her camera to snap the moment that he was lifted onto my chest. It's a harrowing photo because he is limp, head down, and in that photograph I know he was lifeless. He was placed quickly on my chest only to have the cord cut—they needed to get him on oxygen, and quickly. Almost as soon as he was placed on my chest, he was gone again.

For what felt like an eternity, there was only silence. No sound of crying babies or chatting among midwives. Just silence. Even though I felt like I had been in a twelve-car pile-up, I just kept asking where my baby was. *Where is my baby?* Rhian was crying which absolutely sent me into a panic. Then Rhian came over to hold me, and we heard it: the sweet, gurgled shrieking sound of a newborn baby. *He was okay*. His respiratory effort at birth was absent and his Apgar score was woeful, but he very quickly came good. I will be forever in debt to modern medicine for saving my son and bringing him back to me.

My third and ABSOLUTE LAST baby was born on 26 August 2019, at thirty-eight weeks, weighing in at 4 kilograms, with a head circumference of thirty-eight centimetres. The midwife doing his measurements, after we'd had skin-to-skin time for hours, said he had the biggest head she'd measured in her time. Between me and you, my lady bits have never really recovered!

The photos I got from the birth photographer are some of my most treasured pics. They show the strength of a woman, the challenges of childbirth, the traumatic stages and the happy ending. I look at them often and I'm so glad she was in the room with us that day.

As with absolutely every stage of my life this far, birthing my children was so much more than I had anticipated. It knocked me for six and showed me what kind of woman I am. I found strength and resilience I didn't even know I had, even with Copp Luck on my side.

I also know that there are mums out there who sometimes feel robbed of a vaginal labour. They yearn for the hospital rooms filled with grunts and moaning. Over a ball, on all fours, leaning into their partner. They want the pacing and the tears, the feeling of needing to push out their child. Holding their own little alien on their chests. One of my closest friends tried desperately for a vaginal birth after a caesarean. I wanted it to happen for her so much because I knew how badly she wanted it, but her body just wouldn't allow it.

But very few mothers actually get the labour and birth that they've dreamed of. It's okay to mourn the disappointment when those dreams don't come true or those expectations aren't met. Not every woman gets a beautiful birth story and some don't always get the early motherhood moments either—and it's okay to grieve for them as well. I hope me sharing my stories hasn't made anyone feel alone or left out, because behind every birth story that didn't go as expected is the reality of the courage and bravery of women who ultimately do whatever it takes to bring their children safely into the world.

ENGAGEMENT

Expectation: Oh, nothing—just the most romantic moment of my life

Reality: Ever seen Princess Fiona get proposed to?

In my perfect world, I was going to be twenty-three and on a romantic holiday in Hawaii when I got engaged. Preferably on one of the islands like Maui. It would be a warm night, the air would smell like fresh pineapples and I would be on a beach. My prospective suitor would be wearing a tan linen suit with a crisp white shirt. I would go back to our room for an afternoon nap and then be woken by a knock at the door. We were obviously staying at the Four Seasons. A concierge would deliver me a box with a card. Inside would be the most exquisite dress that hugged my youthful pre-baby curves in all the right places and cascaded perfectly over my then perky titties. The card would read: 'Meet me down at the beach at 5.45 p.m.' I would be giddy with excitement, take a shower and make sure I smelled amazing, slip into my dress and make my way down.

As I laid eyes on my partner, I would stop to take it all in through tear-filled eyes. On the beach would be a pathway for me to walk down, lined with red roses on either side. Hot Linen Suit Guy would be waiting for me with a huge smile on his face. To his left would be my favourite pianist, Ludovico Einaudi, who would have been flown in to play 'Nuvole Bianche'. I would have butterflies and be overcome with emotion.

As I walked down the pathway, white doves would be released and I would sharply inhale and feign surprise when Hot Linen Suit Guy lowered himself slowly onto one knee. My hands would fly up to the sides of my face and then across my mouth and I would cry beautifully while a hidden photographer, a videographer and a silent drone captured every part of the moment so we could look back on it for all of time. He would recite a poem he had written himself and finally ask me to marry him. I would feel like I was floating above my body in the most romantic, surreal moment of my life as I shouted, 'YES! A million times, YES!'

I mean, it's almost laughable how VERY differently things played out.

Before we had even told my dad that I was pregnant, Rhian and I had spoken about getting married. I mentioned to him that my mum had my great-grandmother's engagement ring and that I would love to use it as my engagement ring (after having it remodelled, as it was very old) because I loved that it held senti-mental value. It was a diamond ring with a trilogy setting: a bigger diamond in the middle and a smaller one on either side. It sat on a very old, wonky silver band. I remember showing it to Rhian and explaining that it would be nice if we repurposed the smaller diamonds either side of the middle one, trading them in for tiny diamonds that could halo the middle one and then also be used in a very simple wedding band. I had no idea that my mum had already given the ring to Rhian.

On the night we went over to Mum and Dad's place to tell my dad that I was pregnant, Rhian managed to sneak off down the back while Dad was cooking the barbecue and ask him for my hand in marriage. Everything would have been kosher and I would have been none the wiser but Dad had had a fair few reds, his cheeks were flushed and rosy, and he was in the best mood. Not only had he found out that he was about to become a grandfather but this large man was now wanting to make an honest woman of his daughter. It was a lot to take in. So instead of taking it all in, he let it all out.

Mum and I walked down the backyard to join them and the first thing my Dad says is, 'Ohhhh, Sally, Rhian has asked for Amy's hand in marriage—can you believe it?' while my mum is standing there shooting looks that could kill and I am awkwardly trying to pretend like I didn't hear anything.

Fast-forward five months, and by this stage I had no idea when I was getting proposed to. Rhian was pissed that my dad had blown his cover so had played it cool by not proposing *at any point* during my second trimester, when I was ready and looking half-decent. *Keep me on my toes then, fine, I don't even care,* I thought during the third trimester. *But it sure as shit better not be any time soon because now I look like a beluga whale breaching the surface whenever I go swimming, and I'm basically a hairy rectangle on legs.*

Sure as hell, he waited till the hottest day of the year (every heavily pregnant woman's worst nightmare), picked me up from work and drove me down to Redleaf Beach in Double Bay. When I had first met Rhian I was renting an apartment with my girlfriend in Bellevue Hill, and Rhian and I would take a pizza and a bottle of wine down to Redleaf to watch the sunset. We would talk about our future together, and I'm pretty sure we skinny-dipped there once. Not sure if I've mentioned I love swimming nude in the ocean. It was a place of significance to us.

And now here I was, waddling through the hot sand, cursing out loud with a pulsating vagina carrying our surprise soon-to-be-baby. How wild is life? I was super irritable. In fact, I was almost certain I was having Braxton Hicks contractions and/or going into early labour, and was hating on Rhian for making me trek down here when the humidity was a hundred per cent. The thought of a proposal didn't even cross my mind because I was too busy mentally preparing for how I was going to lower myself into a sitting position.

We set up a picnic rug as sweat dripped off my upper lip, and laid out some cheese and crackers, a few beers for Rhian and some soft drink for me. I removed all my clothes and waddled into the water making moo-cow noises and mumbling something about my inner-thigh heat rash and how I just needed this pregnancy to be over. He kept asking me to get out of the water and I kept telling him to piss off. Eventually I surfaced begrudgingly and lowered myself onto a towel, heaving and panting as if I had just competed in a hundred-metre sprint. Rhian started to say a few words but all of a sudden I saw his old flatmates walking towards us, so I started speaking over the top of him, screaming out their names and waving them over. Cue a good thirty-minute chinwag before which, unbeknown to me, Rhian had been just about to propose and was now cramping with anxiety, while I casually lay there like a heavily pregnant dairy cow, chirping away about god knows what.

Once they had said their goodbyes, I turned to Rhian to ask him to check if my entire vagina was still being held discreetly by my bikini bottoms because it felt like there was some flapping-about going on. (Can't make this shit up.) He assured me that everything was still in the vehicle and then grabbed my hand. It was at that moment that I realised something funny was happening. I got instant butterflies in my stomach, more from nerves than anything else, and if I'm being completely truthful, I don't even really remember what he said. But all of a sudden I realised I was being proposed to. Where were the doves? Why wasn't he on his knee? I mean the fact that I was lying down on my side might have had something to do with it. At first I thought he was just doing a Richard Mercer love-song dedication but then, *ta da*, there was a ring—my great-grandmother's precious vintage ring—and he was asking if I would marry him.

I'm not high maintenance, and I knew that the Hawaiian beach, linen suit, rose-scattered sand and flying doves were a little far-fetched (unless you were a Kardashian). So I was floating above my body on cloud nine, and you couldn't wipe the smile off my face. Once I got over the tiny amount of disappointment that he didn't actually get down on one knee, after realising I only had myself to blame, the moment really sank in. I was engaged, on the beach where we had spent so much time getting to know each other, watching the sun go down, pregnant with our heady-love child. It was perfectly imperfect and even though I had so much fluid circulating my body

I looked slightly unrecognisable and the only thing you could really see in the photos that the strangers walking along the beach took for us were my two planet-sized tits, it was *us*. No other proposal would have felt as right or as memorable as this one did.

Was there a photographer hiding in the bushes or a drone flying overhead? No, and I've never been more grateful for that. Was Rhian in a linen suit beaming from ear to ear? No, he was in boardies, sweating for Australia and looking like he was going to release his bowels at any stage. There were mozzies instead of roses and in place of the 'svelte, twenty-three-year-old girlfriend' was a heavily pregnant, panting twenty-nine-year-old lady who had referenced her swollen flaps more than she cared to admit right before the moment went down.

I should mention that being engaged truly is one of the most exciting times in your life. Aside from your wedding, there will be only a handful of times in your life when you can feel excitement and happiness oozing out of all your friends and family, and getting engaged is one of them. You have so much to look forward to and plan, and everyone gets to share in your happiness and come along on the journey with you. Regardless of how the actual proposal went down, the meaning behind it is so much more important. It's a sweet sign of commitment from the person you love and adore.

SOME OF THE FUN WAYS MY FRIENDS HAVE BEEN PROPOSED TO

My girlfriend Leigh's partner organised for a pen of baby goats to be delivered to her mum and dad's house, and when she got in the enclosed ring with them she found out that one of the goats had the ring tied around its neck. This would have been incredibly strange but Leigh is obsessed with baby goats and so this was the cutest proposal ever.

A personal fave of mine is when my girlfriend told her boyfriend she didn't want the proposal to be a big scene, so he jumped in the shower with her one morning and proposed butt naked.

My girlfriend Cate's partner took her out for dinner and was apparently being so awkward (and even a bit rude) that she was convinced he was about to break up with her. Then all of a sudden he got down on one knee and proposed. Seventeen years later they are still happily married.

A lady I used to work with was proposed to in the parking lot of a Burger King where her boyfriend thought he had met her. He hadn't. It was the girlfriend *before* my friend that he was referring to. They are now divorced.

My friend Lauren's partner literally slid the ring across a long table in Bali and said 'Marry me'—and they have been happily married for almost ten years now.

Remember: the proposal doesn't make the wedding and the wedding doesn't make the marriage!

MARRIAGE

Expectation: The never-ending love story with a man who makes me feel like the most special woman on earth every day

Reality: What's romance? Endless farts. Non-stop bickering. Give and take, effort and compromise, and quite literally a full-time job

There were two things that I spent years and years of my childhood obsessing over: who I would marry and what kind of mum I would be. My dream was to be the perfect housewife because that's how I viewed my mum, after all, and she was goals. I'd be the wife who would be waiting at home for her husband, baking cookies, having cleaned the house from top to bottom while wearing a floral blouse and pearls around her neck. Think *The Sound of Music*, *Mrs. Doubtfire* and *Honey, I Shrunk the Kids*. Nine-year-old Amy was a delusional bitch.

Despite the way I personally viewed the roles my mum and dad played, the love that underpins their marriage is all I have ever wanted in mine—a love that will stand the test of time. They have been married for forty-two years now and that blows my mind. *Forty-two years* of putting up with the same person's shit. There have to be some heavy-set foundations of friendship, fun and respect for one another. Or does it become more like companionship?

Some of my favourite memories of watching them when I was growing up are of the way they would always find each other in a room. If there was music playing they would be on the dance floor (you now know where I get it from . . .). They would always sit up in bed of a morning having a cup of tea together, and kiss each other before leaving for work and after work too. For as long as I can remember they would sit down the back of our yard with two deck-chairs and a bottle of wine, watching the sun set and just talking for hours and hours. I would talk to my friends about it, because the idea of being able to just sit without a phone or a screen in your hand and converse for hours on end to the same person you've been with for thirty-odd years would blow my mind. *Like, what are they even talking about? How do they have so much to say?*

My parents' relationship assured me that opposites attract, so I set out to find the yin to my yang—someone who was completely different to me so that we formed a whole. I feel like I went out into the world confidently knowing *exactly* what I wanted from a marriage and almost setting myself up for failure because the thing I was looking for didn't exist.

It's kind of like the way that, before you become a parent, you judge other parents and tell yourself that you are going to be the best parent ever. And then you actually become one. The same applied for me and marriage. There's no such thing as a perfect marriage, or perfect union between two people. Everyone has their flaws, and anything that's worth holding on to requires dedication and work.

After dating my fair share of men and re-evaluating the mythology I'd built in my head around my parents' relationship, I became adamant that the marriage I would have would be a flat, level playing field. It would be all about equality. No one putting it over the other. Things would be 50/50. But of course, I quickly realised that it's never 50/50. *Ever*. There are times when it's 30/70 or 60/40. I also realised that dating people who I deemed to be my 'opposite' wasn't entirely working out as I had planned. Maybe I needed to switch things up a bit and find someone a little bit more like me. While I still think there are a lot of people who are attracted to those who have different personalities, backgrounds and beliefs, ultimately I realised that the most important factor in a successful marriage is compatibility. You can be exactly the same or completely opposite, but if you share the same values and hold the same things in high regard, then the relationship will thrive.

My mum always said to me that when you meet the right person, 'you just know'. *I mean, c'mon, what kind of advice is THAT?* I used to think. With literally every guy I dated, I went through a period of 'just knowing' that he was the one . . . but then time would pass and, sure as shit, he wasn't.

It was only after meeting Rhian and dating him for a short (but intense) time that I knew what she meant. After a few weeks of knowing him, I felt like he had been there all along. I don't want to say that, soon after meeting him, I knew he was going to be the one I married, because that's fairytale-bullshit kind of stuff. But I really did.

We did everything in our own way. I got pregnant three weeks after we moved in together, Rhian proposed when I was nine months pregnant, and we got married in the Hunter Valley when Charli was eleven months old. I know people say this a lot, but our wedding day truly was the best day of my life. There is honestly nothing better than having all of your favourite people in the one room watching you marry the love of your life. I loved every second of it.

The difference between our marriage and a lot of other people's is that they have *time* together early on. Time to get to know each other. Time before they are engaged, time before they are married, and even more time before they welcome a kid into the world. Rhian and I had none of that. We didn't even bang on our wedding night because we were tired parents to an eleven-month-old with an ear infection. The next day, our first day as newlyweds, Charli came back over to our house and I switched right back into the mum role and Rhian the dad. We had six months in total of just *us*, Amy and Rhian. Fifteen months, if you want to count Rhian plus the horny silverback gorilla he dated, which was essentially just *us* plus all my excess fluid. Charli was at our wedding and I cried three out of the six days that we were away for our honeymoon because I left her behind with my parents—not exactly what I had anticipated my honeymoon looking like. So my marriage naturally looks different to my parents' and to my brothers'. But I wouldn't change it for the world. I just thank god we had that first unplanned holiday in the US and Mexico.

Our marriage is stable and consistent and has depth to it. Most importantly I felt a stronger sense of security after tying the knot with Rhian, and this was surprising: I truly had never felt as though my life was lacking anything before I met him. Our commitment to always choose each other, regardless of circumstances, is at the forefront of our minds. While we both know that we shouldn't always rely on each other for all of our happiness, there will be times when one of us will need to step up and support the other person more.

But—and I'm sure you'll relate to this—have you ever loved somebody whose existence also genuinely pisses you off on a daily basis? SAME. The beard shavings in the bathroom, or the shoes he seems to leave in every single place around the house *besides* the shoe rack, make me feel irrationally stabby. I spend a lot of time not really liking the bloke but always loving him fiercely. This is where my expectations of marriage and being in love were really off-kilter. Marriage with the human that you've chosen to partner up with and do life with isn't all sunshine and romance and sensual lovemaking. Love is having a row over something completely minuscule, holding a grudge for a few hours and then folding when he tries to repair it (I rarely fold—stubborn is my middle name—but am working on it). It's letting things blow over and then banging behind the bathroom door. A slap on each other's bums to say 'I love you' and walking away in opposite directions. Love is still getting him a snack when we aren't talking, or not jumping ahead on our favourite show so we can watch it together (because I can sometimes be a spiteful bitch). Loving him is easy. Staying in love with each other is something that we are committed to working at every single day.

My mum and dad always said to me that one of the hardest jobs you'll ever have is your marriage. It's nothing like you expect, and it's something that both parties have to work at every day. They were right. Getting to know Rhian on a much deeper and more personal level kind of took a back seat when I fell pregnant with Charli because it was all about the pregnancy and looking after myself (read: eating meat pies for breakfast and softly bullying Rhian into having sex with me). We got swept up in the excitement of everything and, before we knew it, she was here: we had this beautiful little girl who we were both besotted with. Sure, she might have taken our attention away from each other, but we were both totally fine with it.

There are multiple layers to the way I love my husband, and watching him become a dad made me fall head over heels in love with him even more. Why is there something so sexy about a man holding a baby? Is it because the baby looks so small in their arms? Is it because most men are terrified and they look so vulnerable in that moment? I don't know what it is but Rhian took to fatherhood like an absolute champ. He was there whenever I needed him but he had so much respect for me as a mother. Having Charli knocked my confidence around for a while but after finding my feet and adjusting to my new norm, I always felt like I knew what the right thing was for her. He believed in me and my maternal instincts so much that it helped me flourish in my new role.

One kid was so much fun. We both loved being parents. Rhian and I had spoken at length about how I really wanted to be a stay-at-home mum when we had kids (not realising that situation was going to occur far sooner than either of us were expecting). He absolutely respected that it was something I really wanted to do, and he worked his butt off to ensure that financially we could afford to have me take time off.

Mum always told me to 'not forget about the man' when a baby came along, and to make sure that I was trying to distribute my love evenly. I'm not sure whether my dad was just needy but Rhian never seemed like he needed the assurance that I was there and loved him. He could see what a good job I was doing with raising Charli and he was right beside me, never asking for more but understanding that it really was the most rewarding but also challenging job in the world. We would have date nights here and there but soon enough Bobby came along. Adjusting from one to two kids definitely took a little bit of time but I hit the ground running pretty quickly and we enjoyed our little family unit of four. With each kid, I felt like Rhian and I would have to put in extra effort to make time for us. Our relationship seemed to be overshadowed by other priorities because we were both being pulled in a few directions—Rhian with his work and me with a kid on each arm.

We had only been married for three years when I had Kobe— our third baby in under four years. So, for almost the entire time Rhian and I had been together, I had either been pregnant or breast-feeding. I believe with everything that I have that if I had married the wrong person, the relationship wouldn't have lasted, because three kids absolutely floored me. It pushed me over the edge and I really struggled to even get myself in the shower some days, let alone be intimate with Rhian. Let's be honest, after having three kids in close succession, having sex was like feeding a Tic Tac to a whale anyway, so no one was hitting a home run at this point.

And so we drifted. It was around the first year of Kobe's life that I started to realise how little Rhian and I talked, how preoccupied he was with his work and how rarely we felt close. Most days, we wouldn't talk at all—just a peck on the lips in the morning, then I wouldn't see him till he got home late at night and the kids would be asleep. He has always been shit on the text; he never really sent messages but would always check in with me or call on his lunch breaks. But over the years I had become so preoccupied with our children that I didn't seem to notice how little we communicated during the day. He had had a few promotions at work and threw himself into each new role, so the rift seem to expand without us knowing. The love we had for each other was still there but it was almost like we were both so burned out that neither of us had it in us to put in the effort.

This is *so* common in relationships after kids come along. Whether it's one kid or five kids, they absolutely change the dynamic of a marriage. If you are lucky, you'll have spent adequate time with your partner beforehand so you will more than likely feel ready to divert your attention elsewhere. I felt ripped-off that we hadn't been able to have more time together, while in the same breath was absolutely loving the life and the family we had created together.

I used to say to my mum that 'I don't want to have to ask Rhian to do that—he should just *know*', but that narrative kept us on the hamster wheel of not getting anywhere. I fought it for so many years, but as soon as I realised that Rhian and I are simply not wired the same way, I saw that there were definitely things we needed to put into place to ensure that we stayed in a marriage that was sometimes harmonious. There needed to be soft times. I craved them. So we worked out what each other's love languages were and tried to be more accommodating to each other's needs. My love language has always been physical touch, and when Rhian and I started dating I was the affectionate one. But then I had three kids who craved and loved my affection, so Rhian almost stopped receiving anything from me when it came to physical touch. His top love language is quality time, and I was almost out of that for him, too. Three kids under four had sucked the life out of me and I was depleted on so many fronts. I didn't want to spend time with him. I wanted him to run me a hot bath and then let me sit in the dark with an intravenous drip of red wine.

For a long period there, when we were in the absolute thick of it, we lowered our expectations significantly. For me, as long as both of us *want* to always stay afloat, then I will always be prepared to weather the storm. Communication has become absolutely key. Rhian is marvellous at starting a conversation, and all I need is someone to start a dialogue and I'm off. I sometimes struggle to be that conversation-starter but once the door is open I will emotionally word-vomit everything out.

When Rhian and I communicate, it's like there's violins playing softly in the background and I feel the weight of the tension lifting up off my shoulders almost immediately. When we chat in a civilised manner, I realise that we *can* do it in a really emotionally mature way that truly makes my heart feel at ease. We can listen and respect what the other person is saying, and after being heard we work out solutions (Rhian's favourite word).

It's not all beer and skittles and coming together to have a civilised conversation, of course. A downfall in our relationship, and it usually happens before the communicating part (and it's predominantly because of me), is that I tend to bottle things up and then absolutely blow my stack (I'M BIG B JUNIOR—if I haven't mentioned it already, 'Big B' is my dad's nickname). I can also be a moody psychopath who is incapable of being reasoned with, so that makes life difficult too. (Yes, I'm quite the catch.) I find myself getting unreasonably frustrated that Rhian doesn't pick up the domestic slack when he gets home from work. I find myself getting annoyed that the parenting isn't shared more evenly during the week (not to mention the fact that most nights he doesn't get home till the kids are asleep in bed). I rage when he doesn't put away his freshly washed clothes. Or leaves the toilet seat up. *DO YOU WANT TO DIE, RHIAN?* I find myself having these silly expectations that he should be the perfect man (which is absolutely ridiculous) and when they aren't met, I give him a cold version of myself. I'm a little hostile and temperamental, and not just on the days before my period.

Rhian also has a short fuse and my go-with-the-flow attitude shits him to tears. Where he likes to have his entire day planned out and be out of the house by 8 a.m. on the weekends, I prefer to lie in bed, scroll the internet, cuddle my kids and move at a snail's pace. Marriage is all about coexisting with a person who drives you bonkers and who you can't live without, so the bickering is relentless.

I used to talk openly about the way the dynamics of a marriage can change, especially after having kids, to my childless friends, or to friends who were about to have their first baby. I didn't see it as a fearmongering tactic—more like honest advice that they could think about and absorb (or take with a grain of salt), so that if and when things *did* start to change in their own marriage, they wouldn't be taken by surprise.

When you have kids hanging off your nipples, legs, neck and/or ankles non-stop, a never-ending washing pile and a house that (no matter how often you clean it) looks like it's being renovated by toddlers, you tend to see your spouse walk through the door and handball the kids towards him. I always wanted to be a stay-at-home mum but after Kobe was born I really started questioning my sanity. The days were so long and overwhelming, especially when I had all three at home on my own. Rhian would walk through the door and I would Ctrl-Alt-Delete myself on the spot and try to shut down. That usually didn't end well. There'd be a verbal competition of 'Who's Had the Hardest Day?' (I always won), and then we would argue about tag-teaming kids, responsibilities and cleaning until I went to bed early.

By the time Rhian got into bed, I'd have reached hibernating-bear status and drooled everywhere. And if you think that sounds sexy, Rhian likes to pop off all night long. So every time I'd come back from a kid waking up, I'd pull the blanket up and get hit with the smell of a trapped, week-old dinner like an invisible brick to the face. *Why didn't I know about his flatulence issues until now?* I'd think. *Oh, probably because I had a baby with him after living together for thirty seconds.* I can't even tell you how many times I've decked him in his sleep. Who said romance is dead? Our marriage is thriving.

Relationship Rhian and I used to light candles and make love to music after enjoying a bottle of wine and an uninterrupted meal, during which we would speak about future holidays and how much we loved each other. I'd fall asleep on his chest and we'd wake up at 8 a.m. intertwined with each other. Fast-forward AT THE SPEED OF LIGHT (because that's the speed our relationship moved at) and Marriage Rhian and I weren't even going to bed at the same time. I couldn't even tell you the last time we had a cuddle in bed—I mean a proper, wake-up-on-his-chest cuddle. Candles are now used to defuse a shit smell in the bathroom; music is played for family dance-offs in the kitchen, or to block out kids; and making love is now a two-minute quickie over the bathroom sink. Or with a vibrator, because maybe I gave birth to my internal G-spot during childbirth and clitoral action is where it's at. The two-minute-only bathroom romp isn't because Rhian doesn't get laid very often (but also maybe), but because two minutes is all it takes for Charli to realise she doesn't know where we are, Bobby to set fire to something and Kobe to shit through at least three layers of clothing. It's usually over before it's started, only one person will get a home run (*cough* not me) and then we will peck on the lips, give each other a high five and leave the bathroom at different times.

Free-flowing conversations that you used to have over dinners together will be replaced with incoherent sentences, and you'll lose your train of thought eight seconds in and start wondering if collagen is actually really having any effect on your skin. Sleep-ins will be replaced with 5 a.m. wake-ups and scissor-paper-rocks-offs to decide who has to get up. But, if you have married the right person, you will become teammates and work together instead of against each other. (Easier said than done, and it's still a work in progress.)

All I can say is that when you are deep in the eye of the storm with newborns, young toddlers and kids, and you're feeling exhausted, touched-out and incredibly depleted, all you can really do is hold on, try not to turn a fly into an elephant and, most importantly, *expect less of each other*. You have to know that, for this period, it's okay to not feel as loved-up as you once did. Don't give up because things aren't how they used to be. The house won't always look like this. You won't always be sleep deprived. Know that this is just a passing season.

Put phones down at dinnertime. Find a show that you can both watch together and enjoy something that just the two of you can do once the kids go to bed. Rhian lets me put my cold feet on him at night-time and I don't send him rage-filled text messages when I find his beard hairs in the sink every time he shaves. Every now and again we'll have dinner outside in summer while the sun sets. Or sit on the lounge in winter with a bottle of wine. Rhian will talk about work and I will daydream about the shower I haven't had that day.

Some days I would feel so resentful that Rhian could just get up and go to work. I'd feel resentful of him for just existing sometimes.

For sleeping through the night with his useless nipples, or not pulling his weight. Kids can put an enormous amount of stress on everyday living and it's only normal that you take it out on those closest to you. But just as I am always adjusting to my evolving role, so is he. So I try to remember that, and be more understanding (*try* being the operative word).

Just don't expect things to stay the same between you and your partner when life has changed so dramatically. Things will never be the same. It's not bad, but you do have to learn how to adjust to the constantly evolving roles of parenthood.

I was having a blue with Rhian a few months ago about how complacent we had become. There was no romance in our marriage at the time, no love letters or date nights locked in. We had both really taken our fingers off the trigger when it came to making each other feel good. If you ever wanted to know how much having kids *really* changes your life, here's a helpful and cute comparative essay from my own personal lived experience, which I've prepared for your reference and that I might print out and laminate for Rhian's side of the bed.

Looking a little closer at some of our favourite romantic holidays, here's what these occasions looked like *before* we welcomed three kids into the world (BC) versus *afterwards* (AC).

Valentine's Day Before Children (BC): You lie in bed imagining all the romantic things you plan to do for your partner. Will you cook him dinner wearing your favourite lingerie? (Probably not, because you hate cooking.) But you buy a mass-produced, sentimental card written by someone else, and write in your own lovesick-puppy words about how you've never known a love like this before. You buy a new dress, make sure your hair smells extra good and floss twice. You wear his favourite perfume and buy him a few shirts from his favourite shop. Dinner is somewhere special that holds significance for you both, or it might just be pizza and a bottle of red on the beach while you watch the sun go down. You gaze into each other's eyes and kiss passionately with tongue. If you are feeling adventurous, you might even have spontaneous sex or go for a skinny-dip at night when the beach is deserted. Fellatio to really let him know he's loved.

Valentine's Day After Children (AC): Wake up to obnoxiously loud anal acoustics. He hits you up for a quickie but your libido is holidaying in Mexico so you fight over who has to get up to the baby first. Later, you'll get a text message saying 'Happy Valentine's, babe' so you send one back letting him know that Bobby has just hand-fed Kobe one of his poos and Valentine's Day can piss off. No one gets a card. Sit on the couch moaning like a farm animal because you've begun menstruating. An Instagram memory of you on Valentine's Day six years ago pops up and you repost with 'Together forever'.

Birthdays BC: He sends messages to your girlfriends asking for help to buy you the perfect gift. He sends you little text messages to tell you to keep your birthday free because he's organising something and you're going to love it. You feel giddy with excitement and happiness. He sends flowers to your workplace before picking you up. He nails the present and the card is beautiful. He has organised dinner at your fave restaurant and then afterwards takes you to your fave cocktail bar where he has organised all your friends to meet you. You make love all night because you both have the stamina of pure thoroughbreds and sleep in, waking up entwined in each other's arms.

Birthdays AC: Spend the day bent over the toilet after one of your kids passes on gastro. You sweat for Australia and almost shit out an organ. You survive on Hydralyte iceblocks and your skin turns a shade of corpse. Your husband takes the kids out of the house to give you a break to sleep. Happy birthday to you.

Anniversaries BC: He sends a little gift to your work: it's an envelope filled with lottery tickets and a note that says: 'I feel so lucky to have met you.' You have compiled all of the mushy romantic photos of the two of you and print out a photo book that you can look at forever. You send messages back and forth saying how you can't wait to see each other and how lucky you are to have met. You plan a little weekend away where you walk along the beach hand in hand, enjoy baths together, climax together, etc.

Anniversaries AC: You both forget. Spend the night trimming your pubes in preparation for the two minutes of hushed sex you will have in the pitch black in between children waking up.

Isn't it funny how a moment of reflection can help you to see how bloody lazy you've become in your relationship? I know it means that we have both reached a level of comfort and that neither of us feels like we have to actively work super hard to keep the relationship afloat . . . but it can sometimes be the precursor to a stale relationship, one that becomes a bit boring and monotonous. Having kids is great, sure, but the reason you had them is probably because you and your partner made a choice to bring them into the world—most likely because you were so obsessed with each other and so in love. And yet, once they're here, it's sometimes your partner who you forget about the quickest.

I'm not saying Rhian and I don't make time for each other, but just writing down these before- and after-children scenarios has made me realise that we both need to lift our game a little. Horny goat weed, where you at?

Parenthood will put your marriage in a blender. You have to be prepared to have long stretches of discomfort, and fights over irrelevant things that feel hugely important at the time. It doesn't help that I'm a bottler. And when I'm poked, I will unleash all the bottled-up angst I have about all the unrealistic expectations that haven't been met, and onto the hamster wheel I go.

Rhian, as I'm sure a hundred per cent of people in the world can relate to, doesn't like being spoken to rudely or aggressively. But unlike my mum, who will silently acknowledge my dad's rages (like father, like daughter?) before maturely peacekeeping with him, Rhian will give it back to me. Did I mention that I essentially married myself in male form? We are both headstrong and loud in our opinions—although Rhian is really good at defusing an argument and I've become really good at letting things go. As partners to each other, we are a constantly evolving project. Neither of us is better than the other. (Except that I'm rarely wrong. Just kidding. *Or am I?*) As we've navigated living together and raising three children, I've found that playing to our strengths—not just as parents but as husband and wife—really helps to bring about a full-circle family life.

I do really well with limited sleep, whereas Rhian turns into a moody toddler. So I always did the night wake-ups, and he would always take the kids out of the house early and let me sleep in. Where he is a great cook, I'm a fantastic eater. I cook for the kids and when Rhian gets home from work he cooks for us while I finish putting the kids to bed. I'm good cop (more of a gentle parent) and he's bad cop (more of the disciplinarian). I'm the cuddler; Rhian is the fun one. When the kids hurt themselves, they want Mum. When they want to play Nintendo Switch, they want Dad. I run a tight ship when it comes to schedules and having the kids in bed by 7 p.m., whereas Rhian will still be watching TV with them at 8.30 p.m. given the choice. Rhian is the stress head when certain situations arise (e.g. toddler meltdowns), whereas I can come at situations with a calmer approach. I s'pose as parents you could say there's a little yin and yang going on between us but together we will always try to appear as a united front to our kids, so they know they can't mess with us!

I like to make the bed every morning and make sure the bathroom is always tidy. His side of the room looks like a brothel and he sleeps next to a pile of permanently dirty clothes that he just picks up and chooses from. He doesn't like to hang his towel up after a shower and it makes me want to low-key set fire to something. Another unsolicited tip for making sure you don't end up on the news for murdering your husband: pick your battles. Kind of like you do with a toddler. Marriage is about picking your non-negotiables— things that are important. For me, it's things like communication and being family oriented, like always putting us first, and being honest and truthful. Then there's the other things that I'm okay with being flexible on, like living with a bit of a grub who doesn't often clean up on his side of the bed and *always* leaves his shoes at the front door. I can let those things slide, for the most part.

Now that we have finally found our groove as parents of three, we try to actively make time for us. We organise some date nights. Sometimes they take off and we will have three date nights in three months, and then there will be a period of nothingness for some time. It constantly ebbs and flows. Date nights help to remind us of what brought us together in the first place and hopefully help reignite the flame that burns small, and occasionally goes out, with kids and busy lives. That doesn't happen often but when it does a date night absolutely helps us to reconnect. I'll leave dinner and walk back to the car holding his hand, thinking, 'Holy shit! No wonder I rode the pony bareback with this guy so many times. I'm so into him . . .'

And just like that you remember who you fell in love with all over again.

IDEAL DRINK PAIRINGS WITH MARRIAGE

Hubby has undiagnosed IBS and you've spent more nights than you care to admit being Dutch-ovened?

PAIR WITH: Shot of Chartreuse, a high-proof liqueur that'll kill all your senses, obliterate your nose hairs and burn your tastebuds. It'll taste like shit but it'll get the job done.

Hubby heads out to grab milk and at the same time buys the kids sugary treats for breakfast?

PAIR WITH: Champagne. Best enjoyed alone upstairs while you let him parent solo to deal with the repercussions of his actions.

Hubby cooks a nice meal?

PAIR WITH: Easy-drinking red, like a smooth, medium-bodied shiraz. Sit on the couch holding hands but be sure to drop in not-so-subtle comments like, 'Oh my headache just won't go away,' because you've hit your sex quota for the month.

Hubby leaves plates ABOVE the dishwasher, dirty clothes RIGHT NEXT TO the laundry basket and shoes OUTSIDE the shoe cupboard?

PAIR WITH: His fave beer. Whatever he enjoys most. DRINK THAT. All of it. Or pour it down the drain, or water the plants with it. DESTROY IT.

Hubby tells you he's coming home at 10 p.m. and rolls in at 3 a.m., smelling like a brewery, waking the kids and then trying to hit you up for some intimacy?

PAIR WITH: Espresso martini × 3: hard liquor and coffee are going to help you want to punch him in the face less.

Struggling to orgasm in 90 seconds?

PAIR WITH: A heavy red. Cab sav. Enjoyable for you but it's mainly for him—four glasses in and it should act as a slight anaesthetic. You've now got a three-minute head start.

You go on a girls' night and hubby calls you twenty times in a panic and sends aggressive messages asking how to make the baby stop crying?

PAIR WITH: Rosé, because you are on a girls' night and what else would you be drinking? (Also: although the phone calls are annoying, they also reiterate how irreplaceable you are. Dust the gold from your shoulders and fix your crown.) Follow with a Wet Pussy shot.

By the time this book is out, I will have been married to old mate for eight years. Which is by far my longest romantic relationship! Well done, Amy. But it also does not make me a professional at this whole marriage thing, nor do I really have much long-term history to base my writings off. As with all the other advice I've given in this book that no one asked for, think of it as me sharing what I would with a girlfriend. It's not right and it's not wrong: it's just my opinion and my take on the experiences I've had so far. So if you are my girl-friend and you are struggling within your marriage, here are a few things that I would recommend before you decide to get divorced. (I'd also throw you an epic divorce party if that's the route you want to go down, just FYI.)

- Have intimate date nights. They are the core of your relationship and they will help to remind you of what brought you together in the first place, and why you fell in love with your partner. Visit restaurants that the two of you used to go to. Remember the things you used to love doing together as a couple and do more of them.

- Do things without your partner. Freedom in a relationship, in my humble opinion, is so *so* important. It's liberating. There's nothing better than dressing up and heading out on the town with your girlfriends knowing that you get to let your hair down and then go home to the one you love. You and your partner will share many things together but it's also important to keep your independence. Give each other days away with friends and nights out with mates. It's more than okay to want to be in a loving, committed relationship and also want to be left the fuck alone every once in a while. Those things aren't mutually exclusive!

- Play to your strengths. Like I mentioned, Rhian is absolutely rubbish on broken sleep. It's like having a fourth child, really. But I've always been able to survive on minimal sleep. Like I mentioned earlier, I would do night wake-ups and then pass the baton to Rhian the following morning and go back to sleep while he disappeared with the kids. People play different roles in a marriage. Both are important. He's a master in the kitchen and I delight in feasting on his culinary delights. It's harmonious.

- Remember that fighting is healthy but don't do it like a sixteen-year-old at high school. Try not to be spiteful and don't bring up shit that happened six years ago.
- Do little things to show your love on a regular basis. An 'I love you' text out of the blue can totally change the mood of your partner's day.
- Maintain a steady stream of fresh jokes. A good sense of humour is worth its weight in gold, and so is being able to make each other laugh.
- HUG EACH OTHER. Often and tightly.
- And, as my mum would always say, never go to sleep on an argument. Always talk it out first. (Don't worry if you can't manage this all the time. Rhian and I will blue and then just turn our backs to each other, and he'll be asleep in twelve seconds.)

Marriage is beautiful and loving and messy and sometimes broken, but if you pick the right person and you both love each other, there are very few things you won't be able to work through. My marriage is nothing like my parents', and also everything like it. It shares all the important similarities—such as love, respect and good communication—but Rhian and I run our own race in every other respect: there's a lot of freedom, and we are both lippy bastards who bicker non-stop, and you know when we are both in the room because it's so loud. But, just like Mum and Dad's foundation, we are best friends, we will always have each other's backs and we know how to have a laugh with each other.

There are no right or wrong answers when it comes to marriage. It's all about whatever works for you and makes you happy. Everyone's dynamic looks different. I took from my parents the things that mattered—the core values and learnings that I wanted to apply to my own—but I stayed true to who I am. My dad would never have been okay with my mum, as a mother of three, air-humping to Ginuwine's 'Pony', and that's probably where our differences lie.

I've made a promise to never stop putting in the work with Rhian. Even when he shits me to tears, even when we fight and I don't like looking at him, I will always love him. If we can survive three kids under four, moving house five times, paying off a mortgage and juggling different life roles, not to mention starting a family after only six months of dating (all while still getting to know and understand each other better), than I reckon we will survive anything.

Except maybe menopause. I've heard that's killer.

WHAT'S THE SECRET TO A GOOD MARRIAGE?

Brad and Sally Copp, married forty-two years (together forty-four)

My dad: *Having a good sense of humour and being able to happily laugh with your partner while you're with your kids. If your kids see Mum and Dad happy and smiling, hopefully that will rub off on them. Happy kids equals happy parents and vice versa. Being affectionate and helpful with each other. Doing the little chores around the house and helping out. Not being selfish but thinking of your partner is so important. Also, rubbing some moisturiser into your wife's back after her morning shower is always a good way to start the day, with a chuckle and a laugh and a 'Thank you, dear husband.'*

My mum: *Patience, a sense of humour and always apologising before bed. Never go to bed not talking to each other. Showing each other a bit of affection each day, even just holding hands walking down the street, and most importantly good communication.*

Ben and Jenna, married six years (together eleven)

Ben: *Loving unconditionally and actually enjoying the time you spend with one another (just the two of you). Intimacy and excitement. Having fun together and always putting in the effort to ensure your partner feels that love, and communicating openly and honestly.*

Jenna: *I would say it's loving your partner completely and selflessly, so that means finding a way to love them even when they do things that annoy or bug you and accepting them wholeheartedly for who they truly are. Nobody is perfect but everybody is trying their best. And selflessly being in tune and present, and knowing the ways they need to receive love and the moments they need it in different ways. It could be a kiss and a compliment one time, or doing all the washing and making them their favourite meal another time. And selflessly in the way that you are always their biggest cheer-leader, and love and support them in their individual dreams and endeavours, because you are strongest together when you are both individually whole and fulfilled.*

Matt and Kate, married thirteen years (together twenty)

Matt: *Basically keeping my wife happy. Knowing I'm going to have to compromise first and she was probably 'right'.*

Kate: *I believe the secret to a good marriage is patience and lots of it. You need to have trust and also support each other over the years. Things aren't always going to be perfect and it's going to be hard work. You need to be ready to compromise when things don't go to plan . . . that's mainly my husband compromising but hey, twenty years later and we are still together, so it's clearly working!*

SEX

Expectation: Once you pop, you can't stop!

Reality: Three kids later and it's like throwing a sausage down a hallway

If you're my dad or my brothers, you might want to skip this chapter. For everyone else, feel free to stick around.

I'll spare you all the stories of my sex-filled teens and twenties, but I have never been one to shy away from the topic of sex—even more so since having kids. It's almost laughable what happened to my libido after each baby cannonballed out of me, and I'm determined to normalise it and make sure it's spoken about more often.

From as young as the age of eight I've always been very ... hmmm ... let's go with 'adventurous'. I was always inquisitive when it came to things that felt good on my body. Was it just me or did other people used to hump their pillows when they were growing up? I quickly learned what parts of my body could be easily stimulated and I used to thoroughly enjoy the feeling that followed. Don't put me in a spa bath with jets—I'll be trying to do the splits on the wall of the bath. Lounge chairs? Yeah, I humped them too. My first sexual encounter with another person, which happened just after my sixteenth birthday, was in a very safe environment, with the boyfriend whom I had been gyrating on (clothed) for nine months. It wasn't painful, there was no blood and I orgasmed within a few minutes because I knew how to position my body to ensure specific parts were being targeted.

Cue my love affair with sex and the way it made me feel. Isn't it funny that as girls in school we'd sit in sex education class and be made to fear having sex because it could 'very easily' lead to pregnancy, and yet guys were told that masturbation was a very normal and healthy part of growing up? Masturbation for girls was almost seen as taboo back in the '90s when I was at school, and no one *ever* spoke about it. But old hornbag over here (me) paid no attention to that. In fact, I'm sure that the reason I enjoyed sex so much with my boyfriends was because I knew my body so well. I was very in tune with her and comfortable about speaking up about what felt good and what didn't. I would go exploring most nights in bed and find my toes curling up, and my face going a little numb and getting pins and needles in it. Why did it feel like a dirty little secret, though?

It was always important for me to be with someone who had a healthy sexual appetite—someone who enjoyed sex just as much as I did. Fast-forward to meeting Rhian . . . and lo and behold, not only was he apparently cut from a similar cloth but, at age thirty, he still had the drive of a sixteen-year-old with his very first *Playboy*. I made him wait all of about three weeks before we had sex for the first time and then it was on like Donkey Kong. The words 'constant' and 'everywhere' spring to mind: his house, my house, cars, beaches, the ocean, on holidays, in bathrooms at friends' houses. We even snuck away in the middle of a wedding and had sex in a room that we only later found out was the bride and groom's (don't worry, we're still friends). We were in the honeymoon phase of our relationship, when it's pretty common to be banging like rabbits, but we were rabbits on Viagra who had been eating horny goat weed. It's probably the reason Charli was conceived unexpectedly.

That first pregnancy sent my libido into overdrive and when I wasn't storming through the front door and demanding Rhian enter me, I was hiding in the toilets at work masturbating. It sounds a little concerning typing that out, but the urges were intense and if I didn't see to them I wasn't able to think of anything else. It was like my vagina had blue balls every day and needed a release. Surely that's happened to someone else in pregnancy. Anyone?

After having Charli and transitioning from only having to look after myself to caring for a tiny newborn, everything changed. We waited for the standard six weeks to pass and for my check-up with the GP to make sure my tearing had healed and things were looking slightly less chaotic downstairs before having sex again. I remember the first time we had sex after having Charli I burst into tears halfway through it because it brought up some pretty heavy emotions and feelings. The truth was, there wasn't a single part of me that wanted to have sex for myself. But I wanted to do it for Rhian. I wanted him to know that I hadn't forgotten about his existence and that I loved being intimate with him, but after having an entire human exit the same hole his wiener was now trying to enter, the panic just flooded in and it sucked. *Let's try again in another few weeks*, I thought.

But our sex life was put on the backburner for months and months because I had a newborn whom I was told to wake up and feed every two hours. I didn't even know what time of day it was, let alone where my clit was located. There were parts of me that were acutely aware that we hadn't been intimate in quite some time and I would sometimes feel bad, but those feelings were quickly overridden by my utter exhaustion. I had nothing to give in the bedroom and so, where I could, I would show affection in other ways. We would sit on the couch together and hold hands. We had a sleeping position that we nicknamed P1 (I still don't really know why) where Rhian would hold open his arm for me and I'd curl up into his armpit. There was lots of P1. Lots of forehead kisses and holding hands for the first year of Charli's life while our sex life was slow. And when we did manage to get going, it wasn't remotely adventurous and I needed to use at least a litre of lube because breastfeeding had made me drier than a Christmas tree in March.

It appeared the horny demon inside me had left my body. Not only did I never really feel like sex but I just didn't have those arousing urges anymore. When I was pregnant with Bobby, I became pretty much asexual and Rhian entered into an unofficial partnership with Pornhub. I was so perplexed by how different my body felt that I remember trying to watch porn one day to get myself off, and even though I almost started a friction fire on my clit, I just couldn't get there. WHAT THE HELL WAS HAPPENING? I knew this vessel so well. I knew exactly what to do to get her purring and yet here I was, drier than a desert lizard, with a libido that had clearly packed up its shit and left for a vacation to Mexico. I don't blame it; Mexico is a vibe. But where did that leave me and my still super-horny husband?

By the time we had Kobe, my body felt almost foreign to me. I remember the first time Rhian and I had sex after having Kobe's thirty-eight-centimetre head hovering at my hole's entrance for almost an hour. I felt hollow inside. Like all my organs had been pushed out of the way to house the big baby I made. I was basically a cave. I needed a little grace period to let things slowly adjust and retract back into place. Plus I had loads of incontinence issues to work out before I could have Rhian's sausage lobbed inside me.

Besides, with three very small children, I had the sex drive of a potato. Gone were the days where I would happily jump in the back seat of a car and sit on Rhian's lap. You couldn't have paid me money to have sex anywhere that was remotely uncomfortable. Or cold. Or that required me to take off all my clothes. I turned into something of a starfish. I would still put out here and there—and once we were having sex, it always felt good. It was just that the feeling of *wanting* it had completely disappeared. For four years I put myself last, looking after the needs of my three kids first, and I just didn't have it in me to wax Rhian's sword.

Navigating a sex life with your partner when there are kids involved is tricky. It's something that takes time and simply can't be rushed. When you don't want sex, you need to communicate exactly that. You also need to make space for your partner to communicate what they are missing. If he wanted to go to pound town multiple times a week, then I'd be flipping the bird and asking him to come back with a more reasonable request. But please know that, just as parenting small kids is a season, so is the roller-coaster ride that is your sex life. There can be so many exhilarating moments, but you can also find yourself suddenly stuck at the top of a hill due to a mechanical issue. When you've had a tough day parenting small kids, the last thing you want to do is feign interest in a bulging penis staring directly at you.

Sex is also such an emotional thing for me. Not only did the physical touching stop for me but the resentment built up, and those free-flowing conversations became a thing of the past. I would have been far more inclined to want to jump Rhian's bones if he had helped me bring in the washing and then sat down and we'd just had a chat. About *anything.* I want to talk to my partner and feel like I'm being heard. Based on the qualitative data of many chats with many girlfriends, I've concluded that more often than not, men don't want to simply listen: they only want to offer up solutions to the problems. When I felt like I was drowning in the demands of three babies, I almost hated Rhian. He was also working long hours but, in my head, home life with the kids was always much harder. I actually remember him telling me that going to work felt like a holiday, so my feelings were completely valid. I was more sexually attracted to the Uber Eats delivery driver than I was my husband at one point because I had been harbouring resentment for so long. When he was working long hours and I was three kids deep, intimacy would fall in the 'just couldn't be fucked' basket.

I also have never had a problem with Rhian sorting himself out. The poor guy probably got RSI in one wrist because his wife wouldn't even look in his direction for a few years there. I contemplated buying him a porn subscription once, but I wasn't sure if that would be the precursor to a porn addiction so I held off. (I know some people wouldn't feel comfortable with that and I totally respect that, but we have always been okay with each other watching porn.)

A wise lady once told me that there are lots of ways to help a marriage stay afloat momentarily but ultimately, the two things really necessary for a marriage to survive in the long term are sex and communication (and not necessarily in that order). But I have to agree with her—and you might not, which is fine, because everyone is entitled to their own opinion—because when I wasn't being intimate with Rhian we could have passed as roommates in college. It felt like I was coexisting with my brother. When the sex stopped, so did the physical touch, the flirting, the gazing eyes. The neck kisses. I didn't really notice it anymore, and when I did it felt weird. It started to become our new norm and I felt saddened by it.

Rhian was the most understanding partner on earth (either that, or he was in a fantasy relationship with Jenny_sexkitten69 on Pornhub) and he never really complained. Every now and then he would have a little whinge but it was nothing that would make me feel uncomfortable. In fact, he was kind of just stating the obvious. I had become horny-less. That's not even a word but you catch my drift. I had dried up. My vagina might as well have been a sultana.

If you're lucky, your libido might have only taken off to New Zealand for a ski season, then returned after a few months. Mine had well and truly started a new life in Mexico, married a hot señorita and started a family, and I had no idea if it was ever going to return.

It took me ages to even want to get back on the horse but I noticed that things started to change when Kobe started preschool. It made total sense. For almost five years I had always been at home with a child—or two, or three—and after five years I finally got two days to myself back. So I used that time to do something for myself. It wasn't 'take a poo solo' (but that also felt good). I started pilates. It was there that I slowly started to feel like myself again. I'm not sure if it was the endorphins the pilates set off, or the fact that I didn't have someone hanging off me every minute of the day, but all of a sudden I had a slight skip in my step. And slowly but surely I felt my libido packing up its belongings over in Mexico and starting its long journey home.

It still took a while—because it's a libido, and it doesn't know how to read airport signs—but after a few months of lying on my back and exercising (the only form of exercise I like), my libido walked through the front door and back into my life. Not only did I feel so much better but I started being the one initiating sex. Doing something for myself (even just pilates for an hour twice a week) made me feel like I was coming alive again. Hornbag Amy from 2001 probably won't ever resurface but a more mature, sexually charged mum of three had taken her place. My mojo was back.

From that year onwards, there was a ripple effect: the exercise helped release endorphins, my clitoris came back to life, I fell back in love with self-pleasuring, and it made me want to jump Rhian's bones all over again. After having three children in close succession, most of my internal organs felt like they had been rearranged. My once-favourite position wasn't so comfortable anymore, so we began practising different positions to work out what felt good now. I was also sent a sex toy in a PR package once—it's called the 'Essensual Vibe' but I nicknamed it 'the pear' because that's what it looks like. If you follow me on Instagram you may have seen me mention it a few times. I'm basically their unofficial ambassador and it has absolutely *elevated* my self-pleasure game . . . SWEET BABY JESUS.

For those of you who are back where I was seven years ago, I promise you things will change again for the better. But it's definitely not something that shifts overnight. You will one day start to feel like yourself again, and you'll realise that this too was a season that passed. So ride the roller-coaster (or horsey) that is your libido after children, communicate to your partner if you need time, and say what you want. Listen to your partner's needs and compromise somewhere in the middle. Buy yourself a pear and get reacquainted with your bad self; work out what you and your body like now that things have moved about. Take that new knowledge (and your new toy) into the relationship and spice things up a bit.

FRIENDSHIPS

Expectations: BEST FRIENDS FOREVER

Reality: It's an ongoing evolution

From a young age I always thought friendships were forever, kind of like what I read about in the *Baby-Sitters Club* books and saw on shows like *Friends*: endless smiles, trusting each other with our deepest darkest secrets and always telling the truth. I assumed that friendships started when you were young and finished when you got old and passed away. I thought they were a bit like marriages but in a platonic way.

The reality is, as time goes on, you have less supply of the one thing that really gives friendship oxygen: time. And your friendships change because of this. It means you have friends who stick around for certain chapters and then disappear as life evolves, and friends who turn up for a reason and then leave almost as soon as they arrive. And then, occasionally, you'll have that one friend or group of friends who you met in your youth and who will stay with you for the course of your lives together. These are your rarer lifetime mates.

Friends make your life richer, your laugh louder and your soul happier. They are your tightest vault and should be people you know you can trust implicitly. They lift you up when you are at your lowest and sometimes don't even need to say much to get you through rough situations. Sometimes they are a shoulder to lean on, a hand to hold and company to share a bottle of wine with.

Throughout your life, you will have more friends than you ever expected, but you'll also lose more friends than you ever imagined you would. The friendships that I once thought would never change have all changed. Just like people evolve, so do relationships. Some can leave a bit of a yucky taste in your mouth. Others just softly drift away, leaving lasting memories that will float around your brain for years. You'll be friends with people later in life who would have been your enemies in primary school, and you'll go a decade without speaking to your childhood bestie and barely bat an eyelid. You'll have friends who'll go through one life stage when you're going through the polar opposite, and you'll have to learn how to navigate the differences. You'll have friends who have had the toughest of lives and you'll have friends who endure the best and worst of you— it's not all long lunches and dance floors, and sometimes being a friend means letting someone cry on your shoulder, or listening to them vent yet again about their deadbeat partner, or making them soup when they get a heartbreaking diagnosis. It's sometimes just turning up and sitting in silence with them when you know words won't help, or knowing when they need cheering up and booking in a night to take them out and help put a smile on their face.

My female friendships are without a doubt the most fulfilling and love-drunk relationships I've ever had. They are as important to me as oxygen, unwavering constants in a sea of change—and I couldn't live without them. There is nothing more powerful than having strong girlfriends in your life and I can't stress enough the importance of surrounding yourself with like-minded women.

Spending time with my girlfriends, whether virtually or in person, is so bloody essential for me to maintain my emotional equilibrium and sanity. It's especially important as I age and most definitely when I'm dealing with stress (read: on days that end in 'day'). My friends are my safe space and my voices of reason. They offer a place where there is zero judgement, zero competitiveness and only support. They give me the space to be my authentic, slightly weird self, and we support each other endlessly through our personal and professional challenges. They also allow for breathing space away from home life—away from the kids, where you can just let your hair down and feel a little bit like yourself again.

It's in your adult years that you really start to notice the evolution of friendships. As life's circumstances change and new situations arise, you start to realise who your true friends are. The ones who have been with you since high school might start to fizzle in the background as interests change, partners step in and the dynamic between the two of you alters. You start to understand how much effort is needed to ensure a friendship is thriving and it's important that you embrace the opportunity to nurture meaningful connections with the right individuals. People talk about leaning into your intuition with motherhood and I think the same applies with friendships. You know deep down when you have a friend who truly wants nothing but the best for you; when your happiness is their happiness. Childhood friends sometimes drift off into acquaintance territory and new people appear who make you feel like they have walked this path with you before. It's all part of the evolution.

Imagine friendships as a wacky amusement park, complete with different attractions and rides. In this laughter-filled theme park, we have three types of friends: Reason friends, Season friends and Lifetime friends.

Reason friends: Reason friends are like those thrilling roller-coasters you ride for a specific purpose. They swoop in to show you something about yourself that you are struggling to see. If you are doubting your ability to do things, or you feel your sparkle has faded, these friends will turn up to be your biggest cheerleaders. A Reason friend might become a shoulder to cry on, or someone to ride a certain dip with. Maybe it's helping you survive a maths class or a terrible blind date. For me, these kinds of friendships are special and can vary from being short-term to everlasting depending on how deep you get. Reason friends help you feel less alone; they help steer your neck or help you find your feet. They bring excitement, adventure and maybe a few screams along the way. They will often appear out of nowhere and be the shining light you need at exactly that time, and whatever it is you are going through at that point in your life, they have usually gone through it or are riding the exact same roller-coaster with you. I can think of two Reason friends who came into my life during motherhood for a specific purpose and, thankfully, haven't left my side since. My money is on them becoming Lifetime friends.

After school, I worked in advertising agencies for a few years before I took off to the UK. The boss I had been working with in advertising in Australia just so happened to have left for London a few months before I arrived there. Next minute I'm moving into Lara's spare room and she's my new flatmate. Living in London was a blur, but living in London with Lara was by far the most sensible choice I made during my time over there. She is a good twelve years older than me and, as my dad likes to say, she 'had her head screwed on her shoulders'. I used to call her Little Miss Sunshine because she was a tiny pocket-rocket of joy with a huge smile that could light up a room. She was sensible and mature, and I was a bit of a trainwreck, but boy did we have fun together. She was the reason I even entertained the idea living in London, the reason I stayed, the reason I pushed through the first three months (even though I booked my flight home three times) and the reason I built up enough courage to stay on without her after she went back home.

After Lara left, I moved into a share house with an Irish girl, a Kiwi girl and an English girl and it all went slightly downhill from there—in the best possible way, I mean. There were no rules. No being told what to do by parents or more mature adults. No curfews. We respected one another's boundaries, and would never enter a flatmate's room if that flatmate was not at home. We had a ball.

This was the period when I worked at the pub called Gigalum, and our apartment was right above it. I would bring us home loads of food or we would have a lock-in and just stay downstairs drinking cider till the sun came up. My mum was desperate for me to live overseas and learn how to cook and look after myself properly but I'm almost positive I went backwards. We lived off Sainsbury's microwave lasagne and tinned minestrone soup. The Kiwi girl was a lesbian and had this cute little Canadian girlfriend who would come over and stay, and we would all sit on the couch chatting while she rolled joints for us (sorry, Mum and Dad) and then we would smoke doobies and laugh about the colour of ice cream or something completely ridiculous until we all went to bed and had the best sleep of our lives. Repeat those days and nights for a good two years and yeah, London was a trip.

I made work friends at all the jobs I had. I made friends at the pub I worked at. I made friends on the tube. I absolutely loved listening to stories from other people travelling—what their home lives looked like, where they had visited. Weekends were always so much fun and while I lost myself in the unorthodox chaos of it all, Lara and the girls I met living in that share house were the reason I stayed for so long. *They* were the reason my time living abroad was so memorable.

I also did a lot of travelling while I was over there and it was on these trips that I met some of the closest friends I have ever had. I could list them all but they all know who they are. It all began when I went to the Running of the Bulls in Pamplona, Spain. I was there with another Aussie girlfriend, and a bunch of Sydney girls all came together. From Pamplona we went to Croatia and then on to Ibiza, and before I knew it, some rock-solid friendships had formed. We partied our butts off, woke up in random places and have so many stories to tell that will absolutely not end up in the pages of this book. And thankfully we worked out that we all lived within forty minutes of each other in Sydney, so we could continue the friendship-love party when we all finally arrived home.

All the 'Sydney friends' I made while living overseas brought me deep connections that only strengthened over time. By the end of my time over there I had seen all my new girlfriends in all their forms—at their best and at their worst. Holidaying all over Europe meant the adventures were endless, as was the jetlag, the financial dramas and so on. People played certain roles in the group to ensure everything worked out. Some were more sensible than others, some brought the fun and some were the wild ones! When you live with girlfriends, you see right through to their true selves. And they see your true self too. We always accepted each other for who we were.

The girlfriends I met over in Spain started out as Reason friends: reasons to travel, reasons to party, reasons to live life to the fullest. But they are still heavily in my life now. I was a bridesmaid at two of their weddings and even though we all came back to the motherland at different times, and we live all over Sydney, they still form one of my core friendship groups. Between us we now have nineteen kids. You can't lose multiple brain cells and see all that crazy whacked shit overseas and *not* stay in contact to discuss it often, and at length!

Those Reason friends turned into lifers who I don't always see that often but when we do we hit the ground running. Other Reason friends sometimes just gently fade away, almost like once that reason is fulfilled, you get off the ride. You may wave goodbye, exchange a high-five, and part ways knowing that you had an unforgettable ride together and have some wonderful memories that you'll cherish forever.

Mum friends: Even though they're a subsection of Reason friends, these friends get their very own section because they play such a significant role in our lives. Your Mum friends might be women all around Australia, or even around the world thanks to social media. They are friends who come into your life for a very specific reason, when you embark on a new and exciting journey together. These are the women who join you on life's biggest roller-coaster ride: motherhood. It's all part of birthing yourself into your new life as a mother.

Some Mum friends will be friends you already have; others will be new. Some will be those you meet at the park while pushing your kid on the swing. When you have a child, there will be many new people in your life: you'll be put into birthing groups, you'll attend playgrounds, you'll sign up for playgroups or rhyme time. It's at these places that you'll need to pay close attention. You might need to do a little swiping, as if you're on Tinder, until you meet your people.

I won't go into all the different types of mums there are, but for me, I only fuck with the non-judgemental mums: the mums who are going to pick you up when you've fallen, tell you you're doing a bloody great job, and never *ever* compare you with anyone, judge your parenting skills or raise their eyebrows at how quickly you can down a bottle of red on a school night. Some of my mum's best friends are women she met through playgroup when I was a tiny baby and they are still friends to this day. I can totally understand why. When you have a child it's like becoming part of a secret cult.

When I became a mum I met some of the sickest women (not RSV-sick; I'm talking sick, legendary, wonderful women). Sure, there are undoubtedly a few dick mums who never smile back, or frown upon your style of parenting or the fact that sometimes you let your emotions get the better of you and—god forbid!—raise your voice. But my interactions with those kinds of ball-bags have been few and far between. I'm talking about the mums who give a knowing head tilt when you walk past. The ones that offer to help after you've spent five minutes trying to get into a car that isn't yours and all three of your kids are losing their fucken minds. The mums who give a sympathetic wink when you're trying to pay for petrol with your driver's licence while wearing your pyjama pants, and the mums who give an understanding solidarity nod when you have to publicly reprimand your toddler after they almost decapitate a newborn with a scooter they've stolen at the park. It's like they are saying 'We get it!' just with their eyes—a subtle mum pump-up, a 'You've got this', an invisible high-five.

These are the kinds of women you want in your life when you become a mum, and I met a bunch of them in my mums' group. They have seen me at my absolute worst: pregnant for the third time, with two small kids running laps around me, when I must have looked like a walking shit-stain with zero stamina or personality, and sounded like I only spoke in moo-cow. There are the two mums who I thankfully had on speed dial when I very first entered the motherhood scene: Janey and Jade, two of the girls I met overseas. We were the first in our group to have children—all roughly two months apart—and they were my lifeline. They saved me. We saved each other. Mum friends are absolutely crucial to your survival in your new role. If you are living somewhere remote, you must use social platforms as a way of connecting with other bad bitches like yourself.

One of my closest friends, Bri, is a mum who I started chatting to over Instagram. We had just had our first babies and I could instantly tell she was my type of girl. We became pen pals, in a way; we talked weekly if not daily about what was going on in each other's lives. Fast-forward three years: we'd both had our second children (a month apart from each other), and when Bri moved to Sydney and came round for a swim with her two kids I opened the door to her and we embraced like old friends—when in fact it was the first time we were actually meeting. We then went on to have third babies together. I've never met a woman who is so similar to me in every sense. It's like fate always meant for us to meet—we have been in the exact same places so many times and done the exact same things (her husband is even called Ryan) and yet we had never crossed paths until we started talking on Instagram.

We might live in separate states now, but Bri and I try to make a trip twice a year to see each other. She transitioned from being a Mum friend to a Lifetime friend very quickly. She knows *exactly* how I'm feeling in each parenting chapter because she's living a parallel life next to me and just gets it. She is my confidant, secret keeper, good-time gal and the woman who understands me best. Don't underestimate the power of social media: it brought me her and it can bring you some pretty special people too if you open yourself up to it!

If you don't have a mums' group, just start one yourself, like I did. All you really need is you and one friend and you can start inviting others to join. My mums' group would expand and shrink, and then expand and shrink again as mums went back to work. Even if you don't get to string together complete sentences with each other, just knowing that there's a place to go every Tuesday where there's going to be other adults and you can sip a hot coffee that hasn't gone cold while other mums parent for you can help make you feel less insane in a sometimes mundane and tedious world. I used to go to rhyme time and pick up mums, or even just wander into a park and next minute I'd be chatting up a mum (platonically, of course)—I was always open to meeting new people. It's good to put yourself out there. If you strike up a conversation with someone who is also pushing their kid on a swing, it could be the start of a wonderful friendship—you never know.

Find yourself some Mum friends who make your soul shine from the inside out, who never make you doubt yourself and who pick you up when you fall . . . 'cause you are going to be falling a fair bit (it's a rite of passage when becoming a mum). I bet that a handful of Mum friends you make end up sticking around for life. Either that or they'll slot graciously into the Season ride at the fun park. Motherhood bonds you like nothing else. I literally cried like an overstimulated three-year-old writing this chapter because my three kids have bludgeoned my soul almost to death today and honestly parenting is the biggest trip on earth.

Season friends: These friends are like fun fair rides that appear during certain times of the year. They add a splash of colour and joy to your life. These are the girlfriends who come into your life sporadically and have a wonderful impact on you but then drift off with the autumn leaves. Sometimes it's a hard relationship to process but you just have to take it for what it is. I have had many Season friends who I have become close with throughout my years as an adult. Season friends give you exactly the type of friendship you need at that precise time in your life, and you probably offer them the same kind of solace and friendship in return. Maybe you've moved overseas for a year, or your kids have started at a new school, or you've got yourself a new job, or moved into a new house, or started an entire new chapter at work. They could be your summer buddies, sharing beach days and ice-cream cones. Or perhaps they're your holiday friends you meet while living in Paris over Christmas and who join in on festive celebrations and ugly sweater parties. They might be your party friends, the ones you tore yourself a new asshole with and almost died in fields with (the 'season of chaos', as I like to call it). Maybe they're the friends you went through TAFE with, or the friend you met around the time you had your first child when you didn't know anyone else who was a first-time mother. A lot of old high school and teenage friendships become Season friendships, and these are hard to let go of. Sometimes when you have spent years and years growing up with someone, you automatically go into the default mode of wanting to hold on to the friendship purely because of loyalty and shared history. But sometimes these friendships run their course.

They've gotten you to a certain point in your life, you have absolutely adored and valued them, but you and your friend have simply grown apart.

I've had one friendship like this and it felt like I was going through a break-up for almost six months after we stopped speaking to each other. I felt pangs of sadness, even though we had never had a fight or spoken ill of each other. It was just a friendship that had eventually ended. If you are going through something similar, I hope you know that you will be okay. As one season ends, a new one blossoms, and you might find yourself meeting some new and exciting individuals to share your life with as the weather changes.

My childhood friends were as cute as you could get. My first female friendship, or at least the very first one that I can remember, began when I was about five. Her name was Hannah and she lived in the same street as me. We were inseparable. We started kindy together and spent every weekend finding caves in the bush or having sleepovers at each other's houses. We would run through sprinklers in the front yard on summer days and ride our bikes up to the corner shop to buy hot chips wrapped in brown paper. I remember going through her parents' bedroom when we were about eleven and finding a stash of porno magazines her dad had kept hidden. There were so many different types! We spent hours flicking through the pages, guessing which parts went where. I guess it was like an improv sex-ed class that we took together in her garage. We would make honeycomb on the weekend, and Vegemite toast with Milo hot chocolates every Saturday morning. I couldn't imagine a life without her in it; she almost felt like a sibling, especially because

I never had a sister. We shared clothes and shoes—what was mine was hers, and vice versa.

We went through primary school together and it was only when we got to high school that I noticed a shift in our friendship. She was super smart and a little bit more reserved—I was much more of a tomboy and pretty loud. It was like we had gone as far as we needed to. She started gravitating to a much quieter group of girls who had different interests and I somehow fell in with another group. Our friendship had carried us into our first year of high school and then it pretty much dissipated ... but not in a bad way. There was no animosity. When we were at school we were two different people operating in two different friendship groups, but when we got back home we were Amy and Hannah again, just like it had always been.

I had another girlfriend called Jessica, and we grew up together from the age of five to about seventeen. I would have sleepovers at her place all the time and we would be allowed to stay up *heaps* later than I was at my own house. I was over one night, when we were about twelve, and I remember her older sister was watching the movie *Wild Things*, where Neve Campbell and Denise Richards are in the pool kissing each other. Next minute, I was sitting on Jess's bed after the movie had finished and we tried kissing. First we kissed our hands, then each other's hands, and then each other. I hadn't even kissed a boy at this stage and here I was kissing a girl. It felt weird and kind of naughty but she had really big soft lips that felt like satin pillows, so it was also quite enjoyable.

I remember asking myself afterwards: *Am I gay?* And I didn't really know the answer. But it was all very sweet and innocent, and our friendship felt like a safe place for us to explore different avenues. I'm not sure either of us knew what we were doing and nothing was really ever spoken about, but she was the second good, solid girlfriend I had, and the memories I have of all those summers growing up before hitting my teenage years are what cemented my love for my girlfriends (platonically!).

Another kind of Season friend is the kind you meet at school— although I do know a lot of people who are still just as close to the friends they grew up with throughout school. School is so hard for some people and really fantastic for others, and I believe this all comes down to the types of friends you have. They can make or break your schooling years. High school is equal parts exciting, intimidating and so fucken overwhelming, and knowing your place in the pecking order is crucial. When I started Year 7 and I realised my friend Hannah and I were beginning to drift, I panicked. *I'm at the bottom of the food chain*, I thought. *Who will I sit with? Who will I hang out with at recess and lunch?*

I met a girl in the first few weeks called Amelia, and we bonded pretty instantly in English class. Slowly but surely, little groups started to form and before long we had a modest group of about eight. Everyone was lovely, but Amelia was my person. We bonded over our pale skin, freckles, curly hair and gangly limbs. We were each other's support person at the ugliest stage of our lives. You know that awkward age around thirteen where girls have (or almost have) their period and are crossing over from looking kind of androgynous to looking like a female? (Or was that just me?) When you have tiny nipples that kind of just look like swollen bee stings, and a little bit of underarm hair, and you're slowly growing into your body? We were so awkward and pale. We'd put on blue eye shadow and wet-mousse our hair and go to Blue Light Discos wearing flares and platform Spice Girls shoes and tiny crop tops that showed ninety per cent of our sickly-white midriffs. We thought we were killing it.

My mum fed me devon and tomato sauce sandwiches every day for seven years, accompanied by an apple and some carrot sticks. Forget Dunkaroos or Roll-Ups—a treat for me was a Scotch Finger. But I used to go to Amelia's house after school, and Amelia's house was something else. It was like all my wildest junk-food dreams had come true. Sometimes if I was there for dinner her mum would bring out potato gems and I would damn near shit out a rainbow with glee. But I swear she wasn't my best friend just because the food in her house was elite.

When I was in Year 10, I became close with a bunch of different girls, and I moved between two groups for a while. These were my more rebellious girlfriends, the ones who were more inclined to push the boundaries and who would eventually turn my mum and dad grey. These were the girls I would sneak out of my house with, and we'd laugh for hours and pass out in fields together after drinking vodka mixed with Solo. We'd wake up in each other's beds, our make-up still on, and someone (it was usually me) might have done a wee in a place that wasn't the toilet. We would go to house parties, talk about the boys we had kissed, and every now and again I would try to take up smoking, because back in 2001 it was apparently considered 'cool'. Spoiler alert: I never could, and I've never been more thankful to have sucked (or not sucked very well) at something!

These girlfriends saw me at my most vulnerable. When the weight of the teenage world felt heavy, they were always there. When the smallest things felt *huge*, they were riding right beside me in the hormonal-drama carriage. We went through our insecurities side by side, and picked each other up when there was heartbreak or dramatic goings-on—you know, like when someone has bought the same Hound Dog dress as you. Huge, important things like that.

School gave me so much more than just education, and the friendships I created there were such an important part of forming my identity outside of my family. We learned how to be compassionate, caring and empathetic; they gave me a sense of belonging and of being accepted. There were so many girlfriends throughout high school who made my time there great, but after school we kind of all went our own separate ways. The season of education and homework had come to an end, and so had a lot of the friendships. When we didn't have school connecting us together it required effort from all of us, and the effort just never came.

I know a lot of people are still friends with their high school friends and I think that is so special, but I always knew I was going to move into the city and travel. I WANTED TO TRAVEL SO BADLY. Social media wasn't as prevalent as it is now so it wasn't as easy to stay in contact with each other, especially when I moved to the other side of the world. I still to this day call Amelia a good friend—she's the most beautiful girl with a huge heart and we always make sure we carve out time for each other. I've witnessed her marry her high school sweetheart and have two beautiful children, and although we don't see each other as often as we used to, we can just pick up right where we left off whenever we catch up. Hummus and VB, circa 1996, will live on forever.

Lifetime friends: My Lifetime friends are the special people that I feel the closest to within all the different friendship circles I've been in. I count about five friends in this group, but ultimately the number-one friendship in my life is with my Bezzle, a.k.a. Lauren. Our relationship feels more like family and sisterhood than it does friendship. I once read a quote that said, 'Put more romance into your friendships and more friendships into your romance.' It wasn't particularly revolutionary, but it was the first time I realised that romance doesn't have to be reserved for whoever is putting their penis inside you. It can be with your girlfriends—the ones you have had the happiest, longest and most heavenly relationships with. Lauren and I used to spend Valentine's Day dating the shit out of each other. She made me meatloaf one year and I made Nutella crepes and we ate them on her balcony by candlelight, laughing at dumb shit and all the idiotic men we had wasted our lives dating.

For me, a friendship that can withstand the absolute test of time comes down to two people who are living completely and utterly parallel lives and still making sure they are equally invested in one another's life. I first met Lauren when we were both fifteen years old. We met at a mutual friend's backyard birthday party and I don't even know if we exchanged numbers because I'm almost certain we didn't have mobile phones at that age—maybe it was home phone numbers—but the rest is history. We didn't go to the same school but we spent every single weekend together. When we weren't together, we were sitting at home talking on the phone for hours.

Our relationship was so intense and so wonderful that I'm almost certain people thought we were dating. You know how they say dog owners eventually start looking like their dogs? Well, Lauren and I spent so much time together we started looking like each other too. If she dyed her hair blonde, I dyed mine blonde. If I got extensions, you can bet she did too. We went through our Paris Hilton era together, and then onto our European era in which we dyed our hair dark and coated ourselves in so much fake tan that we were basically walking high-vis humans who could light up hazardous environments. (I'm pretty sure I mentioned this in my speech at her wedding, too.)

All of the trends we went through together—hipster jeans, huge belts, Adidas side-snap trackpants, ironing our hair and plucking our eyebrows within an inch of their lives. We did them all side by side. We got fake IDs and nothing could stop us from going out and spending hours on the dance floor. This was the time of the denim miniskirts and skin-coloured stockings and going into the city to dance all night. I loved a dance floor and Lauren always needed a little bit of liquid courage so when we weren't catching the train, I would drive us in while she drank UDLs in the front seat and then we would dance all night together. If I was kissing a guy, Lauren would be kissing his friend and vice versa. DOUBLE DATES ONLY. You couldn't really ever get one of us on our own: we were a package deal! If Lauren's chicken fillet fell off, I would catch it; if I had an argument with my boyfriend and ran away, Lauren would pick me up. We spent every birthday together and would go away on each other's family holidays.

We are quite different but similar in all the best ways. Where I'm a little loud and crazy, Lauren is calm and chill. She softens me and I bring out her crazy side. We are each other's yin and yang, and our friendship is based around wanting the absolute best for one another, knowing what each other needs without being asked, and deep loyalty. She is the most loyal person I know, the least competitive, the kindest and the most thoughtful, and I'm so glad we found each other all those years ago. When I think about a friendship that experiences divergent phases, it's us. Funnily enough, even though I was always the one who had back-to-back boyfriends and she was single for quite some time, I remember her saying to me once, 'I bet I get married before you'—and sure as shit, she was right. She also went on to say that she always thought she would have trouble falling pregnant. Maybe she has psychic abilities that she's never cared to tap into because she was right about that too.

I was maid of honour at her wedding in Bali while I was pregnant with Charli, and little did I know that would be the start of so many incredibly hard years of infertility for her. While she struggled year after year, I went on to have three children in less than four years, and I felt guilty about each one. She made sure she always expressed how excited she was at the announcement of each pregnancy, but I knew she was hurting. I tried to be there for her as frequently as I could, and I don't know if I always got it right as a friend, but I always tried my hardest. When you have a friend who you know is hurting, you tend to avoid bringing up the subject for fear of upsetting them further. I was guilty sometimes of trying to ignore the elephant in the room, not out of awkwardness or to be mean but because I truly didn't know the right words to say or what I could do to help.

When I fell pregnant for the second time, I remember feeling incredibly nervous about telling her, knowing she had been actively trying for a baby for almost three years at that point. Her response was always the same—happiness and joy—but behind her eyes I could see the pain and it broke me. She deserved to be a mum more than anyone I knew. She loved my daughter like her own and I wanted it so badly for her.

Over six years of riding the emotional roller-coaster of highs, lows, excitement and heartbreaks with Lauren, I learned two things: that you must continue to live your life and share all parts of it with your friends, regardless of the life stages you are in; and that, most importantly, you must *never stop checking in*. I was not the perfect friend, but just as she was navigating her fertility journey, I was also learning how to be the best support person for her. The best advice I can give to anyone who has a friend going through something similar is to just stay connected and stay close to them, even when they push you away. Suggest girly date nights, book a restaurant, get a blow-dry together, have a night out.

Instead of offering Lauren advice that she had heard a million times, or encouraging words that didn't seem so encouraging after a while, I always gave her my silence, held space for her and offered up my comfy (sometimes bony) shoulder to cry on and lean on. I always promised to lock my kids in a cupboard whenever she needed to vent and to find a babysitter at the drop of a hat if she ever needed me. I also promised to not try to figure out solutions for her. I couldn't make her pregnant, but I could take her mind off things and help it not suck for a little while.

For more than five years she rode that roller-coaster, while I was at the other end of the spectrum, trying to navigate life with three kids. Regardless of our differences or the curveballs life threw at us, our friendship always has and always will remain a huge priority in both our lives. It's a friendship that consists of riding through the storms hand in hand and basking in the sunshine together. I honestly can't imagine a world in which she doesn't exist and after all those years of heartache, she now has (by the time this book comes out) three children, and I'm a proud godmother to all of them. I love her and those babies so much I could cry.

From my childhood through to my adult years, I've had some of the most incredible friendships. But as you get older, I think it's normal to slowly start to tighten your circle.

I've seen some of the strongest friendships fall apart. Friends who went into business together have fallen out; best friends who had babies at different times really struggled with the challenges of parenting; friends who left Australia together to go travelling have come home alone. It most certainly is not all sunshine and rainbows. Sometimes a friend's needs can be too high to manage—or, put simply, your expectations aren't aligning.

I had a girlfriend who just didn't understand what juggling three kids can be like. She didn't have children herself and although she tried to be considerate in the early stages, when I wasn't able to drop things with a minute's notice it would infuriate her. Sadly, I had to let go of the friendship, as it wasn't serving either of us well. I think it's quite a common theme when you enter the parenting realm. You desperately want to hold on to the dynamic of your friendship, but your life changes so dramatically when you bring a child into it that if your friendship doesn't evolve alongside it, it tends to get left behind.

The ending of a friendship hurts, but with every door that closes, new ones open. I've found that as life gets busier with work and kids' sport and family commitments, the time that I actually have with my girlfriends becomes smaller and smaller. It's less about quantity and all about quality.

There's no lifetime guarantee when you meet someone you click with, and there is no mould or template that ensures a friendship will last. All I can say is that when you do get a bit older and you narrow in on the tribe of people who set your soul on fire and with whom you feel most at home, you need to love on them *hard*. Friends are the best investment you'll make but you have to make them a priority. Just like romantic relationships, they take nurturing and energy (for the most part!). But they will also fulfil you beyond what a partner alone can give, filling the gaps in your life to give you a full and happy existence. You can't choose your family but you absolutely *can* choose your friends. So choose wisely, love fiercely and never settle for half-assed friendships.

BREASTFEEDING

Expectation: Pop cute baby onto adorable flushed-pink nipple and off we go

Reality: When piranhas attack. FED IS BEST

When it comes to breastfeeding, TV, movies and even my own mum left me with expectations that most certainly didn't always match up with reality. When I thought about breastfeeding, I would think of sun-kissed mothers sitting in fields of daisies with their long, flowy hair softly dancing in the wind. The full bosom would be out and a delicate areola would be discreetly covered up by the soft, pouty lips of a little baby gently sucking away. First you got pregnant. Next step was birth and then it was time to breastfeed. Just three simple steps, really. Right?

When Charli was born and placed on my chest I waited patiently for her to crawl up and place herself onto my nipple. That is what they told me the baby would do in the calm-birthing classes. So I waited. And waited. And she didn't move. She kind of just lay on my chest in her new slimy purple suit not really knowing what the hell to do with herself. And so I assisted and moved her up towards my nipple and plonked her facedown on top of my boob. It felt odd—for both of us, I'm sure. And there began my breastfeeding journey with Charli. Me putting her on my boob and her kind of just hanging around with my nipple in her mouth. Neither of us knew what the fuck we were doing.

It's definitely something that takes time. They just don't tell you those bits in the movies.

Charli was born on Christmas Eve, which meant that the next day there was only skeleton staff on the floor of the maternity unit, and by Boxing Day I had discharged myself because I wanted to be at home instead of sitting in a half-empty hospital. We had spent approximately two days in hospital and Charli had spent approximately 1.8 days facedown on my boob. I was told this was 'cluster feeding' and it's exactly what bubs do to bring the milk in. Never in my life had I felt more like a dairy cow, and I was only forty-eight hours in.

Before we left the hospital, Charli had the once-over from the paediatric doctor and then the midwives. I'll never forget the midwife watching Charli latch, watching me wince in pain, and then telling me that 'if it hurts, she's latching wrong'. But I could see her gulping and I could see colostrum (the very first bit of milk you produce before your supply comes in) around the corners of her mouth when I pulled away. 'Please,' I said, 'show me how to do it so that it doesn't feel like shards of glass are being sucked through my nipples.' But no matter which way they showed me how to latch her, it hurt. It didn't just hurt. It fucken *killed*. I was also told by my midwives that I needed to make sure I woke Charli every two hours to feed her, because she had quite bad jaundice, and had arrived at thirty-seven weeks and was on the smaller side.

Imagine having a baby piranha—all rock-hard gum—latching onto a delicate nipple that had (aside from a gentle caressing and casual tweak here and there) never really been paid a whole lot of attention before. After being tortured every three minutes, it started looking like a battered potato gem. It was those initial ten seconds of every feed when she would latch that really fucked with me in the first week. My toes would curl up, and I'd hold my breath and break out in a sweat, praying to god that she wouldn't unlatch and I would have to start all over again. The cluster feeding almost ended the life of my nipples. How they didn't disintegrate and disappear off my body for good is beyond me. Charli would split them open, they would try to scab up over the next few hours, and then she would latch again and rip the scab off, sucking up milk and blood like a tiny vicious vampire.

My mum told me to sit outside topless to toughen the gems up, and I honestly think that helped. By day ten, the latching pain had eased, and it never returned. I still to this day don't believe that 'it's not meant to hurt'—at least at first. You can't tell me that when you have something attached to your breast, cluster feeding like its life depends on it (which I suppose it does), that it isn't going to hurt (EVEN WITH THE WORLD'S BEST LATCH).

I'll never forget when my milk came in. I was definitely later than the average. Doctors say it typically comes in between two and five days, but mine still hadn't arrived by day six. A midwife had come over to visit and she took one look at my nipples and a flash of fear shot across her eyes. (PTSD, darl?) She told me to drink lots and lots of water but to also go and have a lie down and try to rest while

Charli was sleeping in Rhian's arms. Not sure if she put a spell on my milk or just knew it was coming but I woke up like Dolly Parton on steroids, with angry, veiny, hot-as-hell volcanoes on my chest. They were lumpy and so rock hard that they had almost turned into rectangles. My areolas had changed from digestive biscuits to dinner plates and my nipple could have deadset keyed some cars. *SOMEONE GET THAT BABY ON MY TIT, STAT!* I didn't even care about the latching pain; I just needed some relief from whatever the hell was growing inside my tits. They were bazookas with their own postcodes. I so wish I could post a photo of them in this book, but that might be a little weird. BEAST-MODE BOOBS.

Turns out my milk supply was intense. My letdown could put out a burning house fire from across the road and almost blew Charli's head off, and so I eventually learned how to use her to bring on my letdown and then quickly move her away for a bit so she didn't cop a spraying of milk.

When Charli was about six weeks old, we went to Bowral, a town south of Sydney, to look at a wedding venue. The whole breastfeeding thing was still very much trial and error, but we really wanted to lock in a date and find somewhere to get married. I did everything I could to make sure Charli was fed and in a fresh nappy before we walked into the venue but babies don't give a fuck about your plans—in fact, they love to throw you unexpected challenges the minute you try to be organised. Sure enough, just as I sat down with the lovely wedding coordinator, Charli started piping up. *Please god. No.* I tried the dummy and the shooshing; I tried rocking and cuddling, but nothing was working.

I asked the lady, 'Do you mind if I breastfeed my daughter?'

'Of course not,' she replied. So I whipped out my modesty shield and tried to gather my shit together. Charli was screaming like someone was hacksawing her leg off by this stage (the feeding every two hours had really turned her into a bit of a demanding diva, let me tell you). I started getting hot and flustered. And embarrassed, because every single person who was eating lunch at the venue was turning round to look, and it felt like they were silently accusing me of neglecting my child. Charli's head was doing a three-sixty-degree rotation by this point. She was bright red. I was bright red. I latched the piranha on eventually and could feel the tingles as my letdown came. I tried to move her underneath my boob but she flung her head back, whipping off my modesty shield and exposing my breast. I watched on in horror as I squirted milk right across the table and onto the poor wedding coordinator's fresh caesar salad.

Funnily enough, we did not decide to have our wedding there.

I exclusively breastfed Charli until she was one and then went straight on to cow's milk. Volcano tits aside, I truly loved my journey with Charli. One of my favourite things to do each night was to take her up to sleep. I would light a candle next to my bed and we would sit in the dark and I would breastfeed her while singing 'Somewhere Over the Rainbow'. A Child and Family Health lady told me that you should never feed your baby to sleep but I did for the first six months of her life—and it was honestly heaven!

When Bobby came into the world, I felt prepared. I was a seasoned pro at this. *Baby. Nipple. Let's go.*

The first thing I thought when he was born and placed on my chest was, *Where is his chin?* This might seem like an odd statement to make, but it was honestly the first thing I noticed about his little features. He was so goddamn cute, but he looked like a little turtle for the first two weeks of his life. His latch was pretty good, or so I thought, and he also cluster-fed like a total demon. He was definitely unsettled, though, and I couldn't really understand why. My milk came in and blew up my deflated titties all over again. But I could tell something was different this time. My letdown didn't really ever come and when I put Bobby on to feed, I would never feel that empty feeling I used to have when Charli had finished draining a boob. He was also struggling to put on weight.

At the fourth check-up, the midwife had a look in his mouth and said that she was almost certain he had a tongue tie (a condition that is usually present from birth, it's a short, tight band of tissue that tethers the tongue's tip to the floor of the mouth and can affect eating and speaking and also cause problems with breastfeeding). It had obviously been missed in the checks after his birth. A lactation consultant confirmed that he had quite a severe posterior tongue tie but also that his chin was quite recessed and he had a tiny tongue. When he was two weeks old, we went to have his tongue tie 'revised'—surgically fixed. The nurse used an ultrasound machine on my boob while I was trying to breastfeed and Bobby's tiny little tongue was only flicking the tip of my nipple. He was most certainly not sucking the milk all the way back.

The revision was done and two weeks later we returned to use the same ultrasound machine to see if it had helped. But in some cases the procedure actually sends the baby backwards—and Bobby was one of those. By now his tongue wasn't even connecting with the nipple at all, and if it wasn't for the way I had adapted to feeding him—basically hand-milking myself into his mouth—he would not have been putting on any weight full stop. I had loved breastfeeding Charli and would have loved to have done so with Bobby, but the only thing I love more than breastfeeding is being a happy and mentally well mum.

The nurse who helped assist with Bobby's tongue-tie revision told me point-blank to my face that Bobby would not be able to breastfeed organically. If I was adamant that I only wanted him to have breastmilk, she said, I would have to express every feed and bottle-feed him. I stared at her, searching her eyes for what I needed to hear. She told me to put him on formula. Just like that. She said, 'You have a little girl at home who needs her mum, just like your son does. If you put him on formula, your husband can help out. Your in-laws. Anyone can feed him!'

And yet, I felt a strange sense of pressure to keep trying. My mum is a *huge* breastfeeding advocate. She breastfed all three of her kids and loved it. I get it. I enjoyed my journey with Charli too, but I loved it because it was a mutually beneficial relationship (first ten days aside). I'd had all the time in the world to just sit and feed her. I didn't have anyone else to worry about. Now I had a baby and an almost-two-year-old who needed me.

I tried for a few days to express every feed and bottle-feed Bobby, but the expressing and feeding took so long that by the time he had finished his bottle it was almost time to start expressing again. Recipe for disaster.

So, one night, I thought I'd try giving him a bottle of formula. He was six weeks old and I gave it to him right before bed. When he finished it, I cannot tell you the smile that lit up his face. He started goo-ing and gaa-ing and then I put him to bed and he slept through the night. Even my mum, who thought that formula was the antichrist, saw what it did and how happy it made him, and she suggested I make it a daily thing.

In the same week, I went up to my local early childhood health centre. I was telling the midwife about Bobby's tongue tie, the revision, his poor weight gain and how during the last appointment I had been told he was failing to thrive. I also mentioned that I had started giving him a bottle of formula at night-time and it seemed to be filling his stomach and making him super happy. She looked at me as if I had just told her I was feeding my kid talcum powder mixed with MDMA.

'Why would you do that?' she said. 'You're just confusing him. Of course he won't breastfeed. You have given him a bottle that's easy for him to drink from. No wonder he won't work to drain your breast.'

SORRY ... *WHAT*? I've just told you that my son's tongue doesn't even connect with my nipple due to his anatomy, and that he was screaming after most feeds because he was probably so exhausted from *trying* to breastfeed, and you want to mum-shame me for giving him a bottle to fill up his belly? I left feeling furious— furious that she made me feel like I was doing the wrong thing by my baby. I sat in the car with my hands gripping the steering wheel tightly; I was so worked up I thought about leaving a complaint about her.

What she said didn't have any impact on my mothering journey, but that was because I was a second-time mum, a confident mum, who knew she was a good mum and that her baby was happy and fed. But if the midwife had said that to me the first time around, with Charli, I would have burst into tears in front of her. I would have felt shame and guilt, and I would have gone home and thrown out the formula. By the time I had Kobe I listened to no one. I breastfed him for six months and then switched him to formula. Everyone was winning.

The way I see it, there are some pretty clear camps of opinion when it comes to breastfeeding. The extremists are the ones who can't fathom a world in which formula exists or would ever be necessary. They would rather accept the breastmilk of a total stranger off the internet than give their child formula. When they aren't breast-feeding, they will be pumping round the clock to ensure their supply is plentiful in case they ever need to duck out. I knew a lady once who would point-blank refuse to give her son formula. Even after doctors pleaded with her, she would just have him attached to her boob 24/7 because it was the only time he wasn't crying. He was so malnourished that he ended up being taken into hospital and she was told that if she didn't put him on formula he would eventually die. I know in her heart of hearts she thought she was doing the right thing by him, but when does it start becoming less about the baby and more about the ideology?

You have the enjoyers—those who push forward through the ten-day shitshow and go on to really enjoy the journey. They appreciate that breastfeeding is free and doesn't require any special gear, and they enjoy that you can whip your boob out willy-nilly at any time, anywhere.

Then there's the begrudgers—usually first-time mums who breastfeed because every midwife at the hospital has told them it's so important to do it. Perhaps they have an extremist mum or a group of extremist friends and feel like they can't possibly paint with a different brush. Sometimes they'll have a low milk supply but they'll keep pumping and they'll end up with mastitis over and over again. Their own mental health will take a back seat and they will end up burning out far quicker than the enjoyers, because they aren't doing what is best for them.

Breastfeeding is the ultimate sacrifice of a woman's body and mind. There are so many significant benefits for babies. You are wholeheartedly responsible for keeping someone alive through your breasts and it's a big responsibility if it's one you want to take on. Breastfeeding mums like you to know that they are breastfeeding. It's a huge role, and fair play to them. But the only thing that is as important as a well-fed baby is a mentally well mum. You can't be a good mum if you aren't looking after yourself, and that means recognising when situations don't serve you well.

Formula-feeding mums are often women who have prioritised their own mental health and I salute them. Or they just plain don't *want* to breastfeed. Sometimes there is a plethora of reasons and sometimes there is just one: they don't like the idea of it, or it's not something they've ever thought about doing. My stance on the whole breastfeeding-versus-formula thing is, and always has been, DO WHATEVER IT IS YOU WANT TO DO.

If you want to breastfeed but are struggling, there are so many incredible resources out there that can help you on your journey. If you want to breastfeed exclusively till your kid is four, do whatever makes you happy. If you want to take the tablet just after birth to stop your milk from coming in and start formula feeds from birth, I love that this option exists for you. If mixed feeding works best for you—a li'l from Column A, a li'l from Column B—you beauty!

No two breastfeeding journeys will be the same and each one you go on will have to be personalised to the baby you've just birthed. No one should ever have an opinion on how you plan on raising your baby. And absolutely nobody will ask a kid whether their mum breastfed or formula-fed them as a baby when they get to high school. It's irrelevant. What matters is that Mum is happy and baby is fed.

CAREER

Expectation: University degree, career that I love in the same company until I die

Reality: From advertising to legal, to stay-at-home-mum-ing and social media

When I was five years old, I wanted to be a hairdresser. I loved playing with my Barbies' hair and doing braids in my friends' locks. I just knew I was going to be a wonderful hairdresser. I was a great listener, and we all know that's the secret to being a great hairdresser.

By the time I was ten, I thought doing hair and make-up for a bride on her wedding day was the ultimate gig. Imagine the energy of being able to make someone feel beautiful on the best day of their life! Throughout my school years, my love for hair was still very apparent. I didn't do too badly with my grades, and I loved English, but I never seriously considered another career. My dad wanted me to aim higher and become a brain surgeon or a lawyer, but I barely scraped through Legal Studies at high school so the latter was never happening. Plus, I get instantly queasy at the sight of an open wound, so brain surgery was definitely off the table.

A lot of my friends had decided they wanted to become teachers. Dad talked me out of hairdressing because I had grades that opened up more options, but the truth was that there was never one specific job that really jumped out at me. How did my friend Sarah know a hundred per cent that she wanted to become a business executive at Woolworths? Was she just lying to herself or did I miss a gene that would have given me that confidence and self-assuredness about what my career would look like?

I tried to think of all the things I really loved doing. I was good at netball but even better at rolling my ankles and ending up on crutches. I loved eating but also set fire to most things in the kitchen. I loved making people feel good—hence the idea of hairdressing that lingered—and I *loved* babies. I always wanted to be a mum. I'm pretty sure I even wrote 'Be a mum' in my yearbook when asked what I wanted to do when I grew up. 'Mum-ing' sounded like it would be a walk in the park and seventeen-year-old Amy usually took the easiest route!

I studied a lot of English at school, and I enjoyed it so much more than learning how to dissect a fish in science or learning who invaded who during the First World War in history. I have always loved storytelling and I have enjoyed writing for as long as I can remember. Mum always told me I should write a book because when I was a little girl I used to write in my diary every day. My first boyfriend received a handwritten book from me after I went on holidays for six weeks, and I would write countless letters to my parents when I lived overseas in my twenties.

The obvious move would have been for me to finish high school and study journalism. Instead, I decided I wanted to study criminology. WTF AMY. This was definitely not hairdressing. I used to accompany my dad into the city every now and again and watch him do bail court as a police prosecutor. I'd listen to him tell my mum stories of the people he had put away, which always fascinated me. It was mind-boggling to me to see how people in society acted. But I didn't really want to study criminology: the truth was that I felt lost and clueless about my future, so I had grasped at the nearest thing I had to a career interest.

So there I was, seventeen years old and suddenly high school was over. Then I went cold on criminology over the summer and decided I sure as shit wasn't about to go and do another four years of study at university when I couldn't even pinpoint what elective I wanted to take. I chose to have a 'gap year' instead, hoping something magical would happen and I would instantly know what I wanted to do with the rest of my life.

Spoiler alert: it did quite the opposite.

I started working as a receptionist at a landscaping company that specialised in renovating people's yards. This is hilarious in hindsight, because I have killed every single plant I've ever owned and don't even know how to start a lawnmower. But hey, I was there to answer phones, not bring anyone's yard back to life. This particular chapter in my life opened up my eyes to what it was like to (1) not study, and (2) EARN MONEY, and whooooooooa, daddy, did it feel *good*. I was on about twenty-eight grand a year and I felt like P. DIDDY. I pitied those media and communications fools tirelessly studying away while a hectic deposit of $550 dropped into my bank account each week. *Drinks are on me, guys!* After realising the freedom that came with earning an income, I made a decision then and there that the workforce was for me. University felt like repeating high school over again but having to pay for it, and the thought of doing one more assignment made me want to violently heave. No, I made up my mind. I was a working gal now . . . I just needed to get out of *Burke's Backyard* and find an industry that was more 'me'.

After some soul searching, I set my heart on advertising. I started as a receptionist in a buying agency and felt like I had found the EXACT INDUSTRY I needed to be in. There was an in-house DJ. People wore bright colours and congregated in the kitchen and threw parties at lunchtime. One guy had a parrot that would sit on his shoulder all day long, and half the staff operated out of huge love sacks with laptops on their thighs. It was fun, super cool and definitely my vibe. When a role for a media buyer was advertised, I took a leap of faith and applied for it. They took a punt on me and the rest is history.

I spent almost nine years working in advertising in a few different agencies. I went from the buying side over to the creative side. When I was living in London I worked in buying agencies and when I was back in Sydney I ended up in TV production in two different agencies. Some of the best years of my life were working in advertising—so many great friendships, so many cool parties, way too much drinking and memories that will last a lifetime.

In my mid-twenties I hit another crossroads in life—one that I brought upon myself. As I mentioned earlier, a Kiwi boyfriend asked me to move over to Auckland for a few years to live with him. Long story short is that it was a total disaster and six weeks after moving over there I returned to Sydney with my tail between my legs. I was twenty-six, unemployed and back living with Mum and Dad, having clearly chosen the wrong path to venture down. I felt lost and confused and a little bit angry at myself. It was like I was back in Year 12, finishing my HSC all over again and not having a clue about what to do with myself next.

Or did I?

After enjoying a bizarre unemployed summer, I tried to poach my old job back from the girl who had replaced me. Turned out she was even better at the job than I'd been and I had shot myself in the foot. My girlfriend Jade reached out and said her sister-in-law was looking for a paralegal as a maternity-leave cover in an in-house legal team. Six weeks of unemployed life had been great but I was pretty eager to sink my teeth back into some work and start earning money again, so I went in for an interview. Fortunately for me, Copp Luck always seems to find its way into my job interviews. I can fumble my words and respond to questions in German or with answers that make absolutely no sense at all because I'm so nervous; I can have my fly undone or call the interviewer by the wrong name; but I've never gone for a job interview and not got the job. Did I get it because I'm super smart and they were blown away by my interview skills? Doubtful. Was it because I'm clumsy and a bit awkward but seem really friendly and it's only a maternity cover so how bad could I really be? MORE LIKELY. So there I was. A paralegal. Kind of like I had made my way towards that criminology degree, right? Legal? Crime? No?

The office culture could not have been more different to the culture in advertising. Where in my previous job, people had ridden around the hallways on motorised scooters and had cans of beer at their desks, this corporate role was stale as hell. You could literally hear a pin drop in the office. No one spoke. Everyone looked the same in their grey suits and crisp white shirts, and everyone kind of looked like they were on edge all the time. *What fresh hell is this?* My boss would only speak to me via email. It took him almost six weeks to come out of his office and address me like a normal human being, and I think he was so taken aback by my cheery disposition that he would sometimes stick his coffee order on the outside of his door so he didn't have to deal with me barging in every morning to chat. *No one chatted.* I had so many friends in advertising but here I was with these work-bots who seemed to have zero personality. So I made it my mission to break them all in. I was going to crack all these stale pieces of toast and we were going to bring this office alive. *Somehow.*

If there's one thing I can do (aside from make an incredible Mars Bar slice), it is bring the party. Or get you in the mood to party. Or make you make decisions that you'll more than likely regret the next morning. And no, I didn't sleep with anyone in the office, but I definitely brought them all out of their shell a bit!

I distinctly remember my boss asking me to come into his office when the maternity cover was drawing to an end. He said to me, 'You aren't that great as a paralegal, but you bring something else to the team that is priceless, and we'd love to offer you a full-time job here.' And that, my friends, is the greatest backhanded compliment I've ever received. I went on to work there for another two years. It was a little boring but the pay was great and once I got everyone out and about, drinking and dancing and letting go of their inhibitions a bit, they all turned out to be legends who had just been a bit guarded. And regardless of what my boss had to say, I always got my work done and I definitely learned a lot about the legal world. Some would even call me a contract wizard.

It was during this time that I met Rhian and then, shortly after that, faced another crossroads—one that didn't even really seem like a crossroads at the time because ultimately it was all I had ever wanted. I fell pregnant.

I had recently been poached to another in-house legal team. Kind of a big deal in the paralegal word, you know . . . I was three weeks into the new role, and was absolutely elated about it, when I pissed on a stick in a toilet cubicle at work. And there I was. WITH CHILD.

Not only did I almost pass out, but I had absolutely no idea what the right thing to do was. Did I tell my new boss, who I thought was amazing, that I had accidentally got knocked up? Did I wait until I got to the twelve-week mark and then tell her? Was I keeping this baby? Was I really having a baby with a man called RHIAN? (Okay, I didn't really ask myself that one.) But I felt like I had arrived at a bizarre intersection that had about five roads shooting off from where I was standing. As with everything in life that takes you by surprise, I really had no idea what to do. If you've read the pregnancy chapter you know which road I ventured down, and the fact that it led me to my toughest job of all time: MOTHERHOOD. Where the staff are overworked, underpaid and so goddamn *tired*.

But there's an entire chapter coming up on this season of living—plus I'm still employed by my tiny bosses—so we'll skip that for now. Next up: social media.

After having Charli, I was like almost every other new parent on the planet and took to social media to share aesthetically pleasing photos of her and talk about the overflowing love I felt. And that was most certainly not a lie, but within the first week of coming home from hospital with a tiny, jaundiced alien that liked to be attached to my breasts every twenty-five minutes, I started to realise that there were no accounts on Instagram that spoke about motherhood in a more truthful light.

Why did no one talk about sleep deprivation feeling like a form of torture, or let me know that I would cry for almost a week after giving birth for absolutely NO REASON at all? I'm talking standing in the middle of Woolworths looking at a pile of bananas and just bursting into tears. *A heads-up? From anyone?* No one warned me that the anxiety I would feel before going to bed at night would be so debilitating that I couldn't even eat dinner sometimes because I knew night was coming and darkness meant I was about to be tortured by continually broken sleep. I wanted desperately to know that this helpless feeling wasn't just me—that it was normal.

This wasn't a lightbulb moment where I thought, *I'm going to be the first woman on the moon (read: Instagram) who is going to tell it like it is!* No, it was just me choosing to write from a more relatable and honest perspective and hoping that in time I would meet other mums who were finding new motherhood a similar experience. It was almost like I was putting out a mating call for mums who also had no fucken idea what they were doing but were putting one foot in front of the other every day and hoping for the best.

I was dogshit, deliriously tired for the first six months, and maintaining a sense of humour was what kept me alive. So I wrote, and when I would write about motherhood and my new role as a mum I would detail things in a raw and entertaining way. And lo and behold . . . absolutely nothing happened. I was just your everyday mum spitting truths about the relentlessness of parenthood while being sickeningly in love with my daughter.

But slowly, people started to follow along. My inbox started filling up with the most wonderful messages from like-minded women. We were in the trenches or boarding the roller-coaster, and it was scary and uncertain but we were all doing it together. It was nice to not feel so alone. I became online pen pals with these women, and they truly saved me on some of the hardest days. Social media became a wonderful safe haven, somewhere I could just be myself. I was more than happy to be vulnerable and to open up about how hard I was finding things, because as soon as one person starts talking, everyone else opens up.

So that's kind of how I fell into the whole Instagram content-creating realm. People used to use the term 'influencer', which everyone now says that they hate. I hate it from a marketing perspective, but I absolutely hope that I have influenced people in different ways—ways that made them feel good about themselves or let them know that it is okay to not *love* parenting all the time.

Fast-forward a few years and I'd taken everyone on the journey of my next two pregnancies and births. Remember how I mentioned that I loved storytelling? Well, Instagram kind of became a livestream of my journey. But I did it in a very honest, tongue-in-cheek, 'if I don't laugh I'll cry' way that people seemed to really gravitate towards. A friend would tell their friend ('She has three kids but still goes out and dances like a twenty-one-year-old stripper? YOU MEAN WE CAN STILL HAVE A LIFE AFTER CHILDREN?') and that friend would tell another friend, and the word spread that there was a chick on the 'gram who wouldn't shy away from saying all the things most of us mums were thinking.

I am more than okay with taking the piss out of myself, and out of Rhian and my brothers and my family too. We are all as self-deprecating as they come. People can gossip and talk shit about me till the cows come home but more often than not I'll be one step ahead of them, and will be saying it about myself already.

I've always tried to see life through rose-coloured glasses. I work on the things I can control and I try to laugh off the things I can't. I most certainly have absolute SHOCKERS some weeks but I show up on the 'gram for them as well. I was an open book from the minute I joined the platform till now, so you'll see me bossing parenting, out with my girlfriends looking fly with an entirely new face on, then looking like a sewer rat while all three children are handing my ass to me. It's almost like tiny snippets of a reality show that absolutely nobody asked for!

And then the opportunities to monetise the platform came about. While most people were supportive, it's funny how some people get weird when a woman starts earning money. I'd spent hours and hours on the platform for years and years, sharing the highs of motherhood, the lows and everything in between, but the minute I used the paid partnership tag, people weren't happy.

When brands started getting in contact with me and asking me to promote certain products, I took the role very seriously. After not working for almost five years and not being able to contribute financially to our family at all, I thought, *Why not jump at this opportunity?* So 'content creator' became the next job I fell into completely randomly and organically.

I understand the lack of respect there is for the role because I used to think it was a bit of a joke too. I can only say that now, having been on both sides of the consuming and content-creating fence, it really isn't as easy as you think. Bear with me while I give you a brief overview of why social media advertising can be a fantastic resource for brands, and how much work and effort goes in behind the scenes to bring it all to life. And PLEASE FEEL FREE TO SKIP THIS PART IF YOU COULDN'T GIVE A FUCK ABOUT SOCIAL MEDIA.

If you are a decent content creator, you put a lot of time and effort into understanding a brief and the key messaging a client is trying to get across. You work with brands that you know and trust, and you promote them wholeheartedly to a community that trusts your opinions and knows you wouldn't sell them up the river. Having worked in advertising and TV production, I can tell you that social media is one of the best forms of advertising you can engage in when trying to promote your business. (That's especially true for you, small businesses!) You will be able to reach a larger and more tailored demographic than you could buying a spot on TV or on radio. Marketing with the right content creator can singlehandedly make your business take off and build from there. Traditional forms of marketing don't work as well as they used to, and those who aren't leveraging digital marketing may be missing out on key strategies that can increase their performance and get their business better results.

I put thought and effort into each brief I get. Some have super-strict guidelines, some like to give me creative control, but I always try to bring the brief to life in a way that I know will land well with my community—with humour, or with information that I think would be helpful. I try to keep aspects of my personality throughout it. Even if my community doesn't give two shits about the brand or what I'm advertising, I hope that they can respect that I've put in the time and effort.

It's like being my own in-house advertising agency. In a traditional set-up, brands go to an advertising agency, and the agency has a creative look over the brief and writes up a few concepts to present to the client. Now I do that.

Then the agency brings the chosen concept to life, which is what I used to do when I worked in TV production. The absolute chaos of bringing a TV commercial to life would take days and sometimes weeks—lighting, sound, props, talent—and now I do all that too.

Then the video is sent over to the brand for approval. If you are lucky, it will be approved first go. If not, tough titties—you have to shoot again!

Once approved by the client, in the ad agency set-up the video is sent to a copywriter, who then writes a script to complement said video. I do that too.

And, finally, the video is uploaded by someone from the buying agency who has bought certain time slots and knows when the demographic they are after are most active . . . and live it goes. This is also my job.

Plus, I then make sure I'm engaging with my audience and answering any questions they might have. The best thing about working with a content creator is the ability to directly track the return on investment from your marketing campaigns, which means everyone wins if you've picked a good one!

However, the expectations I had of turning this platform into a workplace and earning an income from it were *so* far from what it is really like. Full disclosure: I thought it would be easy, and I thought the lovely community of women who had followed me this far would be okay with it. I thought others would be happy for me. Some are happy for me, but with growth comes hate. As my account grew, it brought in all different types of people . . . and with them came a whole lot of unsolicited opinions. When you are a friendly mum who prides herself on writing back to everyone and returning messages, all of a sudden things can get very overwhelming. You never want a message to go unread or un-replied-to, but when your account starts growing it's physically impossible to keep up with the messages, the questions, the people seeking advice, the people looking for help or companionship. It's impossible to stay on top of it all and so I just have to do what I can when I have the time.

Work structure aside, what you really need to understand about having a platform is that you need to be okay with putting yourself out there. You need to be okay with people forming an opinion of you, scrutinising your every move and passing judgement, whether that judgement is right or wrong.

For every ninety-nine people who follow me and are lovely, there will be one who won't like the way I live my life and what I share. They won't enjoy seeing me on a night out or the fact that I love to dance. They'll make comments about the dynamic of my family, or how I raise my kids. They won't like that I've turned the platform into a profitable workplace, even though I work really hard for the brands. They will want to see me fail. They will hate what I stand for.

Unfortunately, these people are usually the loudest. You need to develop a thick skin really quickly, but above all that you need to be confident in who you are and not worry about the opinions of others. Which I can assure you is so much easier said than done. It really is a two-sided coin, or a double-edged sword: it's given me the flexibility to be present for my kids where I can and allowed me to help support my family financially as well. It's allowed me to tap into my creative side and, funnily enough, my previous two jobs played a beneficial role in the job that I do now. But the job definitely comes with a dark side and unless you can live without inhibitions and avoid giving too much energy to those who don't matter, then it will slowly eat away at you.

And there we have it: a little overview of content creating on a social media platform. I can assure you it's not for the faint-hearted and it really is a lot more work than most people think.

After I began content creating on Instagram, tiny side streets started appearing. Down one of them I started writing a monthly article for a website called The Latch. It was a great outlet because my captions were always word-limited on Instagram but for the website I could write and write and write.

A little further up then down another tight little laneway, I was offered the opportunity to host my own podcast. My first response was: *No. Honestly, who wants to listen to the sound of my voice, and do people even listen to podcasts? Surely everyone else is only listening to '90s R&B when they have their AirPods in . . . no?* But after some thinking and chatting to friends, I thought, *What do I have to lose?* and went in to record my first ever podcast. Doing a podcast is scary, and doing one on your own is goddamn terrifying. Having no one to bounce off was almost impossible, even for someone like me who can talk underwater. The very first podcast I did took me four gos to get right. I sounded like I was choking on a hair ball and/or being put to sleep with gas in the very first one I recorded. The second one had way too many pauses, and stories that went around roundabouts, and the third was basically in German because I was still so nervous that I jumbled up all my words and nothing made a whole lot of sense. By the fourth attempt, I had calmed myself down and managed to get the trailer out.

My very first guest on the show was none other than my dad, and by the third episode I was talking candidly about my sex life and what that looked like after having three kids. My podcast, *Beyond the Likes*, is one of the things I'm proudest of. It's a totally unfiltered and even steeper deep-dive into who I am as a person and what I have to offer. I don't profess to be a master at anything—merely an everyday mum, wife, daughter, sister and friend who doesn't shy away from taboo subjects and will happily open up and talk about absolutely anything.

I had recorded a podcast every single week for about a year when I hit one million downloads, and to say I was proud of that accomplishment is an understatement. Every week, I made sure I got a podcast out—rain, hail or shine. Whether I had to do it sitting in my wardrobe hiding from my kids, or out the front of mums' group sitting in my car sweating profusely in thirty-plus-degree heat, I always made sure an episode of *Beyond the Likes* was out every Wednesday morning at 4 a.m. I now have a second podcast that I do with parenting educator Gen Muir called *Beyond the Chaos*, which is predominantly about raising children, and knowing that I get to turn up and chat candidly with someone who I love and respect makes the whole process that much more enjoyable!

If you had told me at seventeen that I would end up being the host of my very own podcast and a co-host of another, while working with wonderful brands and engaging with an incredible community of women in an online space, I would have laughed in your face and asked what you were smoking. And yet here I am.

Life truly does have a funny way of twisting and turning when you least expect it. You can follow a metaphorical life map and be convinced of your future, but roadworks and infrastructure are always changing around you. Planning your future and working towards a career is wonderful, but those goals are also made at a particular moment in time, when you are embedded within a personal and social context of hopes, dreams and predilections, and sometimes they don't reflect what your reality will be—even if they help create it in different ways.

My career path could not have turned out to be more different than what I had once imagined. I've been choosing left or right at every crossroads I've come to and hoping for the best. My career constantly evolves, as do I as a person.

Does anyone ever really know whether they are making the right choice or not? Isn't that the biggest mystery of life? I think that's what keeps it exciting! I often sit back and wonder whether or not I made the right decision at particular points, but in fact every single turn I have made has led me down a path that I have loved (even when the roads were hard to understand and painful to follow). I'd still go down them again, because they have brought me to this very place.

THINGS I WOULD SAY TO MY
TWENTY-YEAR-OLD SELF

Dear twenty-year-old Amy,

Damn you are cute when you are feeling overwhelmed. I honestly can't stress enough that you really have nothing to be overwhelmed about at the moment. Life is great for you! I know how heightened your emotions are and how you feel like the weight of the world sometimes sits on your shoulders but I just need to say: don't sweat the small stuff, babe.

I don't want to build up your expectations too high, but you'd better buckle up, girlfriend, because the next ten years of your life are going to be the absolute best. The bee's knees. The duck's nuts. You are going to take 'Living Your Best Life' to another level.

You will find independence and your backbone and slowly, over time, you will start to flourish into a proper grown-up. Kind of. Between you and me, though, the cooking skills never really take off. Thankfully we marry a man who can cook, so we good.

But, with hindsight, there are a few things that I wish to give you a heads-up about—things that won't change the course of your life but may save you some time, money and stress, and help you to appreciate the little stuff a bit more. So here we go.

- No one, and I truly mean NO ONE, thinks you look better when you abuse solariums. It's not hot to put your skin through that kind of trauma and neither is the smell of burning skin (which you will carry around with you for five years). As a now-thirty-seven-year-old fossil, I so appreciate you covering your face every time you use a solarium, but honestly, you can't botox your neck or your decolletage, so you've totally done me an injustice. At 37, your neck now resembles an uncircumcised penis, just saying.

- When you are on the pill and still making your boyfriend use a condom, I can assure you, getting the morning-after pill as a precaution is not necessary. The stars really do all need to align in order for you to get pregnant, despite the fearmongering we ingested as teenagers. That said, I absolutely commend you on your STI safety measures.

- Do not step back into a past relationship when you already know how the book ends. Trust me: it ends the same way every time. This might save you an unnecessary heartbreak in your mid-twenties.

- ACCEPT YOUR FRECKLES. I know you are still so self-conscious about them, but they aren't going anywhere. One day you will love every single one of them and so will your husband, but right now you are fake-tanning like a crazy lady and look like a large piece of poo with legs.

- Do not date the South African rugby player you will meet in London. I know he's hot but he has a wife in South Africa. You won't know this until she tries to kill you.
- Enjoy the way your body looks. You are a regal thoroughbred in comparison to the years to come. You are sleek, smooth and tight-skinned, with perky tits and a firm undercarriage. You can jump on a trampoline like a magical unicorn. Enjoy all the midriffs and the way your knees bend gracefully without cracking. Spanx and panty liners will soon be your best friends and you'll have to take an anti-inflammatory before hitting the dance floor in 2023 (but don't worry, that won't stop you).
- Here's an important one: *really* enjoy those child-free years. ENJOY THE SHIT OUT OF THEM. 'Just because' after-work drinks? Why the fuck not. Nine a.m. sleep-ins? For the love of all that is holy, SLEEP. Sleep until you can't sleep anymore, you young beast. Two loads of washing per week? YOU ARE LIVING THE DREAM. Long hot showers? Take two a day! In the future, you'll be lucky to get one every three days. Weekends away with your boyfriend? Sex without lube? Who even are you. Poo on your own? These really are the best years of your life. Hot food? On your own plate, with your own utensils? While no one fingers it? LAP IT UP. Eat with reckless abandon.
- Travel! Take this one seriously. TRAVEL THE WORLD, GIRL. Pack your tooth-flossing bikini and book the next

flight to Croatia. You can find accommodation when you get there. Sleep on the floor in a motel. Don't sleep at all. YOLO your entire trip.

- Enjoy a little alone time. Read the books, get the pedicures, take yourself to the movies. Spoil yourself rotten. Self-care is vital right now for you to be okay with sitting at the bottom of the pecking order in years to come. When you hit your thirties there's going to be some hard years; pedicures will become a memory and you won't get your undercarriage waxed for at least two years. I know, I know, you don't believe me but it's true. At one stage, you will have Dumbledore's beard growing between your legs. Don't worry, you come good after your third kid turns two. Did I mention kids yet? You are having three of them!

- Hangovers? Enjoy lying in bed with pizza and movies. Soon you'll learn that the number of kids you have directly correlates to the severity of the hangover. Hangovers will soon become less a sign of a good night out and more a unique form of torture.

- Just know that after all these years, meeting your partner and having your own children will change your life (literally and figuratively) in ways you can't even begin to imagine, and you will experience a love that can't be put into words. Also, chaos. *So much chaos.*

You'll also be forever grateful I got this letter to you so you can enter your thirties and motherhood with not a stone unturned. Nor will you have a single shred of regret. (Except for maybe that one short-term boyfriend you had in Greece who gave you chlamydia. You can leave that stone unturned.)

Love,

Amy xx

BABIES

Expectations: They just sleep, eat and poo

Reality: Like a slap to the face with a 14-kilo barramundi

You know when you were a kid and your parents' friends would come over with their new bundle of joy? Then they'd only let you hold the baby while sitting on the lounge and it would hover over your lap while the adult supported its neck? That was my first initiation into newborn holding (and I wasn't even really holding one). As I got older, there were freshies everywhere (that's what we would call a baby that was fully cooked and just out of the uterus). I think the freshest one I saw was when my best friend's sister had a baby. Lauren and I used to go over most weekends and 'help' babysit her.

This baby was different to the ones I had seen in movies, on the covers of magazines or in the arms of women at the park. This baby cried. A LOT. In fact, the only time she wasn't crying was when she was being held upright and you were walking up and down the stairs with her. The minute your bum touched the fabric of a lounge, she would start crying again. It was quite full-on and she required more attention than either Lauren or I had realised babies needed.

I remember leaving that house some days feeling exhausted. Lauren's sister seemed a little bit off with the fairies and was quiet a lot of the time when we were there, which I clearly paid no attention to. But all that babysitting practice made me feel confident that I was going to boss the whole motherhood gig. Even more so because Lauren's sister's baby was quite demanding, and surely mine wouldn't be like that.

HA.

Let me start by saying this: not a single book, birthing class, conversation with relatives or babysitting/nannying job can *ever* prepare you for the birth of your own child. Sure you can study up till your little heart's content, but when they land earthside, HOLD ON TO YOUR HAT, DOROTHY. Shit gets real. Not even Copp Luck would save me.

Here's what it's really like; here's the truth that no one warned me about. In one split second, you go from being a single adult in the world to a *mother*. You are responsible for a tiny purple alien that is half yours and half your partner's. You are also bleeding profusely, potentially stitched up, and feeling like you have been hit by a freight train and could sleep for a solid month.

Having told absolutely anyone who would listen that all I'd ever wanted to do was become a mum, I was very taken aback in the first moment I met my daughter. Alongside the sheer relief, there was no lightning shock of intense love. Was it the thirty hours of labour that had rendered me emotionless? I wasn't sure, but when Charli was put on my chest I didn't really feel anything. She was lukewarm and slimy and had big bulging eyes that were looking up at me.

I waited for the tears. Or the emotion. I expected to feel an internal explosion of love, but nothing came. I felt a void of emotion. Some people talk about this, and some people don't. Personally I don't think this response is anything to be ashamed of—I was simply in a state of shock.

Charli started crying almost immediately and I tried to navigate the memories in my brain to figure out what to do when a baby cried. But my brain must have shut down during labour because I had no fucking clue. I wrapped my arms around her and tried to keep her warm, but still the crying continued. Was I holding her right? Was she meant to commando-crawl up onto my nipple? Was I meant to stop them from cutting the umbilical cord so quickly? Why was she crying? There were so many questions that I couldn't seem to work out the answers to, or even bring myself to ask aloud.

It was like having a concussion except my head wasn't sore—my vagina was. The tiny alien lying on my chest was making blood-curdling noises that sounded like she was choking or drowning in something and all I could think was, *WHAT THE HELL IS GOING ON?* Because my waters had broken early and my strep-B test results weren't back yet, the doctor treated both of us with antibiotics to be safe. I was hooked up to a drip and so was my sweet girl. We were in a public hospital and because I really like to throw myself into the deep end, I'd sent Rhian home at the end of the night so he could get some rest. You know, because he'd done so many hard yards during that labour. But also because I needed him to be chipper in the morning and so forth.

So there I was, with my six-hour-old daughter. Just the two of us. It was terrifying and beautiful. All the emotions I had wanted to feel that moment she landed on my chest finally started to happen, now that it was just the two of us.

Recovering from that first birth was hard. I had both internal and external stitches, and going to the toilet felt like I was passing volcanic lava. They wouldn't let me leave the hospital until I had done my first poo and I felt more nervous about that than the entire giving-birth scenario. How could I possibly bear down and push out a turd? My entire insides would surely fall out. I had to really work myself up for it. Prune juice, apple juice, all the juices. I eventually needed a laxative and when I slowly lowered myself onto that porcelain bowl, heart racing a million miles an hour because I thought I was definitely going to bust my stitches, I broke out in a rancid sweat and thought I was going to pass out. It was the first time I had ever experienced anxiety and it was about releasing yesterday's dinner. How times had already changed.

With the tests and checks done, my undercarriage still intact (just) and both of us girls having released our bowels, we were set free into the world. I'm pretty sure Rhian drove 30 Ks an hour under the speed limit the whole way home and I sat in the back next to Charli because not being right next to her felt terrifying. What if she stopped breathing? This was a question I would ask myself almost hourly for the next three months.

I'll never forget walking through our front door at home and thinking, *Right, what do we do with her?* Unbeknown to us, for the first six to eight weeks all they really do is sleep. So far, expectations were matching reality. Still . . . cue me checking on her breathing every twenty minutes, licking my finger and holding it under her tiny button nose to make sure she was still with us.

Charli was a pretty great sleeper from the get-go. She would cluster-feed all day and only wake once during the night. But the first time a midwife came out to do her checks, she told me Charli had some breastmilk jaundice and, because she came at thirty-seven weeks and was a little on the smaller side (she really wasn't), I should feed her every two hours.

Now, here's one thing that Third-Time Mum Amy would never have done: she would *never* have listened to that advice. I don't think it was misinformation or that the midwife was trying to make my life harder—she was just passing on the information she had been taught—but as a rookie mum, I took everyone else's word as gospel. So from that visit onwards I would wake Charli every two hours through the night to feed her. What resulted was a very chubby newborn who was awake way more during the night and sleeping for most of the day. This midwife had literally flipped the day/night situation on me, and I ended up a nervous wreck because of it.

I tried to do the 'sleep when the baby sleeps' thing during the day, but I have issues sleeping at the best of times: since well before Charli came along I had needed a pitch-black room and a contoured supportive pillow because I have the neck strength of an eighty-five-year-old. I was also still recovering from the birth. I felt like every muscle and bone in my body had been put through the ringer; my vagina felt like it had been put in a blender and I'm almost certain my asshole was still turned inside out from all the pushing. My stitches got infected and I had to go back on more antibiotics, which then gave me thrush, so honestly it was really not the year for my undercarriage. She had been through some trauma.

The days, weeks and months all blended together and I lost my grip on the concept of time. I finally understood why Lauren's sister had been walking around like she'd had a concussion for the first four weeks of her daughter's life. I didn't even know if I had showered most days, let alone brushed my teeth. Rhian had taken the first two weeks off to be with us and help, but by this stage Charli was sleeping all day and I was roaming around the house like a headless chicken, moaning about the stitches and leaking milk everywhere. My letdown was aggressive and Charli was also a spewer, so our one-bedroom apartment soon turned into a kind of vomit dungeon—like a Baby Bunting store after a hundred bin chickens have gone through it.

I remember taking Charli to the doctor multiple times to ask if she had a lifelong condition in which she slept more than she should. I also took her to two different doctors after I had videoed her crying because I was convinced there was something more sinister going on. To say I wasn't a super-chilled mum would be an understatement, but is anyone really ever that chill with their first? There wasn't anything wrong with Charli; she was a happy, chubby little baby who made me look like an idiot by goo-ing and gaa-ing at the doctor's while being checked over. Turned out the sleepiness was normal, as was the hysterical crying from 5 p.m. to 10 p.m. every night. Witching hour, they like to call it. But mine never went for an hour, it went for what felt like an eternity. I knew that babies cried, but I was not prepared for this.

I searched the web daily for a baby manual but for every piece of advice I found there would be an opposing view, and every piece of advice said that following the opposite advice would be detrimental to a child's development. Let them cry it out. Never let them cry it out. Feed on demand. Feed every four hours. Don't rock them to sleep. Always cuddle your baby. WHAT IN GOD'S NAME WAS THE ANSWER?

The thing about motherhood is that no one knows. *Seriously*. Not a single person on earth who has had a child knows what the right or wrong answer is. It's a 'choose your own adventure' every time. It's about doing whatever you need to do to get through those early years. If you want to read *Save Our Sleep* and put them into a routine from birth, do that. If you want to live in the woods and breastfeed round the clock and co-sleep, do that. However you want to parent, the choice is yours. The problem is that once people have chosen their path, they frequently like to push their methods on to others in an almost evangelical way.

In our society, motherhood can often be represented in unrealistic, idealised ways. If a parent's expectations are very different from the reality, it can make it harder for them to adjust to life with a new baby. Some of my friends set themselves unachievable goals and then became overwhelmed, found it difficult to cope or felt as though they had failed. I prefer to set no goals and just go with the flow. It's been my method at almost every stage of my life. Wing and a prayer and a little serving of Copp Luck. Oh, and a sense of humour—it's IMPERATIVE for survival.

But it's also helpful to remember that adjusting to life with a new baby is enormously testing and it can take time. Having realistic expectations of what motherhood can involve can help you better adjust.

Becoming a mum for the first time was not only NOTHING like I expected it to be or could have ever prepared for, but it was honestly one of the most challenging things I've ever done. Not in a torturous Tough Mudder way (although, sometimes yes) but in a way that pushed me to every limit I had. It is a time-consuming, labour-intensive, emotional task, one that means a fundamental shift in your identity as well as often difficult physiological changes. I loved my daughter more than life itself, and I felt like my heart would burst sometimes when I looked at her, but there were also feelings of anxiety that were sometimes mixed with boredom, or resentment towards Rhian.

I lost myself in those first couple of months. Motherhood changes you instantly. It's like a slap to the face with a 14-kilo barramundi. In the first six weeks you won't remember to wash your hair, eat or prioritise your own needs. Sleep deprivation, feeding and nappies will fill the long, formless days. Your anxiety will rear its head, and the fear of getting it wrong or somehow not looking after your newborn properly can sometimes consume you. Feelings of panic, ambivalence and uncertainty can take lots of getting used to.

The deeply penetrating love you feel for your child is all-consuming and makes you feel like someone has propelled a rocket straight up your ass and sent you on a one-way mission to THE MOST INTENSE LOVE YOU'VE EVER FELT. Coupled with the fact that you are now responsible for this tadpole, which makes you incredibly protective, the overwhelming love is one of the greatest feelings in the world (and the most terrifying). Romances come and go but the intense love you feel for your child will have you hooked for life. It isn't just intellectual or cultural—it's a basic part of our make-up as parents.

Because of said love, I pushed through the sleep deprivation and the fact that Charli almost split both my nipples in half in week three. There was an overwhelming sense of despair and confusion about why everything felt so hard. I was beyond exhausted, in pain and I found myself asking, *What have I done?* I feel like these conflicting feelings have existed for as long as mothers have existed, but there's a taboo around associating them with motherhood, never mind with being a 'good mother'.

And so I buried them and I tried desperately to emulate my own mum. I wanted to be the mum who cooked only organic meals and never allowed the baby to stay awake longer than the advised 'age-appropriate wake time'. My house would be pristine, and I would still always put in an effort with my appearance. Rhian would be greeted with a warm smile and the smell of freshly baked cookies every afternoon, and my libido would bounce back with a vengeance. And then there was the reality: I could barely stay awake to watch a TV show with him in the first six months, and what's a libido?

In the mumming space, over time, I felt like I could have won a Most Improved award. By around six months, we were going to rhyme time at the library, and at home I would read to her—even when she had the neck control of a slinky and had no idea what I was saying. I would link our pinkies and stare at her little face, losing hours and hours of the day watching her facial expressions and thinking, *So this is my new normal.* Everything was at a much slower pace and a little boring, but every time she smiled at me or laughed, I knew this was exactly where I wanted to be.

I would go for morning walks, and catch up with girlfriends for coffee dates. I would take Charli to the park and we would have picnics under a tree while the sun was out, and when it came time to feed Charli solids I would always prepare the freshest food and then freeze what I didn't use for the following day. I was kind of starting to feel like I was nailing a new role I had been hired for. Slowly and surely I had found my rhythm.

I met other mums who had similar parenting styles. And I also met Dalai Lama mums, and competitive mums, and among them all I found the joyful, warm, text-you-back-at-ungodly-hours mums who made me feel seen and less alone by sharing their vulnerability. Together we would help each other through the difficult times and find joy and amusement in the aspects beyond our control!

My body had changed. I didn't fit into my old clothes or have any desire to walk in eleven-inch heels. My skin was looser, I had battle scars where I had grown my daughter, and a cheeseburger that had definitely been upsized to a Big Mac. Well, that's what it felt like, anyway. I never went back to the body I had before childbirth, and yet I felt like leaving it at the door signified so much more than just becoming a mum. I had an air of confidence about me, an air of I JUST CREATED A HUMAN WITH THIS MAGNIFICENT VESSEL. I felt more at ease than I had in so long. Charli adored me at every moment throughout the day and sometimes the smallest people can have the biggest impact. She showed me all the things that I would sometimes struggle to see in myself. She made me feel soft and warm and firm in all the right spots. My hugs felt like home to her, and my forehead kisses fixed everything. She made me feel like I was enough for her, exactly as I was, and it was a rebirth of my confidence and a time of knowing my self-worth. In her own way, without even knowing, she really did make me feel invincible.

Looking back on my initiation into motherhood, I can tell you now I had an easy firstborn. At the time I honestly had no idea; it was all I knew. Everyone's first foray into motherhood is overwhelming, but I didn't have a reflux baby, or a baby who didn't sleep. I breastfed easily with an abundant milk supply for a year, and Charli took to solids like a champ. She slept through the night from pretty early on and was overall very chilled. She was what they like to call a 'textbook baby'—did all the 'right' things, supposedly. The cocky bitch in me naturally put it down to my own mothering techniques (but of *course*!), and I'll be the first to admit (don't hate me) that I got a little bit high on my own fumes.

I'm still not sure whether it was because I had Charli first and she lured me into thinking that my parenting techniques were the shit, or whether it was karma leering at me and holding a sign that said 'YOU GON LEARN TODAY', but my next two children were absolutely *nothing* like Charli—more like two wild, testosterone-packed chimpanzees that had been set free in a zoo, each of them with the emotional regulation skills of a potato. Boy, did I get my ass handed to me.

As babies, Bobby and Kobe were both pretty good. They excelled at sleeping and when I was getting adequate amounts of sleep, I could handle anything. They slid right into the eat, shit, sleep rhythm, and life was hectic. Bobby was the happiest little babe, and the first twelve months of him earthside were utter bliss. He smiled at every twist and turn, slept like a husband and accompanied me all over the place. Because I couldn't breastfeed him, other people played a more hands-on role in helping me feed him, including but not limited to Charli, who at two years of age became my little sidekick and part-time helper. Never mind that she was still technically a toddler herself—she grew up quickly to help raise the wild boys with me.

Kobe was a little dreamboat newborn too. He arrived when Bobby was only twenty-two months old and had just begun testing the boundaries. Perfect timing, really. Being induced with Kobe and giving birth to a man-baby meant he didn't come out starving and slept for Australia from day one. He was large and in charge, and thank god because he got manhandled like a hot potato from the minute he was born. Nothing bothered him, and he would giggle hysterically at his brother and sister's antics, or watch on adoringly with an eagerness to join in. His first year of life felt like it went by in two-and-a-half months. I rarely got to soak up the newborn stage with him because Charli would be crying over bumps in her hair and Bobby would be trying to torch the house. I think the most alone time we ever got was in the hospital after he was born. I told the midwives that I had a preschooler and a toddler at home, and they told me to stay for as long as I liked.

Your first day as a parent will be like no other day you've ever had before. The aesthetically pleasing photos you see of mums holding their newborns in hospital won't even scratch the realistic side of it, or convey how intense and sometimes overwhelming (while also exciting) your new life will feel. Bringing your first baby home and learning how to navigate life with a three-day-old will be intimidating and so eye-opening and you'll look at mums who have more than one kid and think of them as real-life superheroes.

As a mum who has only just survived three toddlers, the baby stage feels like a walk in the park in comparison. Might have to write another book after having teenagers though—I've heard they give the newborns, babies and toddlers combined a run for their money.

To anyone reading this book who is a first-time mum, here's some unsolicited advice that I wish someone had given me before I had my kids.

Remember the person you were before kids? The one who used to love going to the gym after work and then meeting up with their partner for dinner? Maybe you were the one who loved cruising through op shops with your bestie and then having lunch. Or you woke up early in the morning and went for an ocean swim, then a sauna, before the sun came up. Did you spend six hours at the shops and actually try everything on? Or book weekends away, or travel the world? Okay, keep that person in your mind as you read on.

When you have a child, the first couple of months hit you like a pile of dog shit lit on fire. Everything is all a bit trial and error and you'll find a new (much slower, barely-get-out-of-first-gear) pace as you try to find your feet in your new role, and holy shit you have an entire human to look after. *Where is the manual?*

Motherhood may be everything you ever wanted, but why does leaving the house feel so terrifying? How come Stephanie, who has twins, was out at a first birthday party forty-eight hours after giving birth? Social media will either fill you with a false sense of security or will make you feel like you are not good enough. You might try to keep up appearances and attend ALL OF THE THINGS but, if you are anything like me, the baby blues will get you good and you'll end up locking yourself in the toilets and crying for half an hour because you feel so overwhelmed. What is this new life that you signed up for?

The weight of responsibility will bear down on your shoulders twenty-four hours a day. Keeping a human alive truly is a full-time job, with no sick leave or days off. There are no set hours at which you can check out and arrive back when you are well-rested. That's why making time for yourself is of the utmost importance.

If you are reading this as a first-time mum, you'll wonder: *how?* How do you leave a baby who needs you so much? Who craves your touch and your smell? Who only settles in your arms? As a third-time mum, I can promise you that a few hours' reprieve is worth its weight in absolute gold when it comes to motherhood.

I remember a midwife saying to me, 'If only third-time mothers could birth their first child'—oh, the things you would do differently. Only as a third-time mum can I tell you that prioritising yourself pays dividends in the way you will raise your child, and that looking after your mental health is paramount and will help you more than you can imagine on your journey. Stepping out for a few hours to regain a sense of calm, peace and sanity will do wonders for you as a human being but also as a mum!

I rarely left Charli in her first year of life (except for my thirtieth birthday party, which I attended for a few hours and had to leave early because my tits almost exploded off my chest, and for my own hens' night). I was riddled with guilt at the thought of leaving her, even though my mum would beg to take her for a few hours for me.

I was so attached and so protective. Every part of me ached for her when I wasn't there. I was her everything. But, in the same breath, I wasn't looking after myself. I put all my needs and wants behind hers, which is so normal for a first-time mum, but it was only after having Bobby and being able to step away for a few days or nights that I realised two things: that my kids enjoyed the break from us (granted, they were always cared for by loving family, friends or babysitters), and that recharging the batteries turned me into a LORD parent, with a refilled glass of patience. It also made me miss my kids like ABSOLUTE MAD.

I often felt like a target, with ALL the emotional arrows being fired at me at once. Sometimes you're fine and things feel manageable, and other times it's terrifying and overwhelming and your whole body aches from being everything to everyone. Stepping out of your role momentarily to regather yourself is an absolute gamechanger.

Now that I've become a total professional at self-care, I probably take the piss a little bit too much, but I'm very lucky to have three sets of incredible grandparents who love to spend time with my kids— and my kids love to spend time with them. Now, I spend my time encouraging other mums to prioritise themselves. Remember that person you were before kids? Let her carve out some time for herself every so often. That doesn't mean you have to go out drinking and dancing like an eighteen-year-old with an intact uterus like I choose to do. It could mean spending the morning at the beach or reading a book. Or going for a massage with your best friend followed by a long lunch. Whatever it is that fills your cup, do that . . . and do it often. Not only will you feel so much better, but your kids will reap the benefits of having a recharged, happy and well-balanced mum.

TIME TO RECHARGE

Here are some things you could consider doing for yourself if you are a first-time mum:

- Book yourself in for a massage.
- Arrange to have a brekkie date with a friend for some one-on-one bonding time, and leave baby with your partner or another support person.
- Take yourself to the movies.
- Grab a book and a picnic rug and go lie under a tree and read for a few hours. Just on your own.
- Go and get a manicure or pedicure.
- Go for a walk along the beach.
- Organise a lunch with a group of girlfriends, and all get dressed up for a few hours.
- Take your mum shopping and do some retail therapy together.
- Book yourself in for a blow-dry. Even if it's just so someone else can wash your hair for you. That scalp massage is never a bad idea!
- Pop on a podcast and go pound the pavement.
- Outsource a few things. Get a cleaner. Order some ready-made meals. Take your washing to a laundromat.

TODDLERS

Expectation: A wonderful few years of great cognitive, emotional and social development

Reality: STRAP YOURSELF THE FUCK IN

I didn't really know what to expect when I was moving out of the baby chapter and into the toddler one, but I sure as shit wasn't going to have a kid who backchatted, threw themselves on the ground in public and behaved exactly like a toddler . . . no, no, *no*. My kids would listen to what I said. They wouldn't push boundaries or do age-inappropriate stuff. They would be like the von Trapp children in *The Sound of Music*. They would eat whatever I cooked or they would go to bed hungry. They would transition to big beds seamlessly and they would sleep in those beds for years to come, before moving out of home as adults. Bedrooms would always be kept clean and tidy, too. No one would watch iPads or be spoiled and carry on like brats. As my grandpa used to say, 'Children should be seen and not heard.'

For full transparency, I am yet to come face to face with the teenage years, which I have constantly been warned about, but toddlers were almost the death of me. They were absolutely

NOTHING like I had anticipated. My seemingly manageable role as a mum of three quickly turned into a chaotic clusterfuck. Never before have I experienced such disorder. My downward spiral began when Bobby was 18 months. He had always been a super busy kid, but all of a sudden we were hitting the terrible twos (something I had unwittingly bypassed with Charli) and my tiny, blond-haired, blue-eyed, Viking-looking kid was suddenly very angry.

I used every single parenting technique I had used on Charli with Bobby, but—surprise, surprise—he wasn't the same kid. Where Charli would surrender after a little hug, Bobby would start throwing out headbutts, clenching his tiny little fists and screaming into the air. Kobe spent the first four months of his life in a baby carrier face-planting into my boobs because I needed both hands free at all times when Bobby was around. Trying to keep clothes on the kid was almost impossible, and his favourite thing to do when he wasn't trying to stretch his foreskin over his shoulder was to shit in his nappy and hand the poos to me. Usually in horrific places such as Woolworths next to the vegetables, or while I was filling up with petrol. Thankfully he was usually somewhat dehydrated so they would hold their shape and I could dispose of them while they were still intact. (Add that to 'Stories I Never Thought I'd Be Telling'.)

If I had to compartmentalise it even further—and this is purely from my own lived experience—I would tell you that toddler boys and toddler girls are quite different. Sure, they are both going through similar age-appropriate emotional and cognitive developments, but compared to my boys as toddlers, Charli was a Tibetan monk. Everything about having Charli first deluded me into false impressions. She would have an occasional meltdown here or there but it was nothing that I would shy away from. Her throwdowns weren't overly aggressive or loud, and they were few and far between. Charli would cry over the colour of the plate I served her dinner on or not being happy with the outfit I had picked for her. Bobby, though, went through a particularly angry phase and would yell and scream most places down, and Kobe went through an equally aggressive one in which he would use his body as a weapon and try to take people out.

When Charli was about eighteen months old, we lived in a townhouse complex. Next door was a lady who had a boy the same age as Charli. We would often go to the park and have play dates together. Her son was very sweet but his temper was like nothing I'd seen before. When he didn't want to leave the park or couldn't express himself the way he wanted to, he would lose it and start swinging left hooks and headbutts. Naturally, like the deluded imbecile that I was, I put it down to my neighbour being too soft with him. *She's obviously not disciplining him right*, I thought. *She needs to put consequences in place to ensure that kind of behaviour never happens again.* Because OF COURSE she wasn't—her son was only eighteen months old! But there I was, like a smug son of a bitch, with my daughter holding my hand as we left the park, mentally patting myself on the back because I figured I was clearly doing something right. The baby gods took one look at me and thought: *Oh gosh, this bitch is getting FAR too high on her own fumes. We need to send her a little care package.*

And out came my two boys, both of whom have swung left hooks at me too. I've copped scratches, shin kicks and pinches, and I've carried both of them out of shopping centres under my arm like footy balls. I've lost count of how many meltdowns we've experienced in the middle of Woolworths where I've just had to wait while they rolled themselves down the aisle like cheese sticks. Because I wasn't a lord parent and nor was I better at mumming than any another mum. That mum from our townhouse complex was doing everything right. She was staying calm in an otherwise uncomfortable situation. She was not losing her cool. If anyone needed a left hook in that park situation it was Amy with the one daughter. I got taught a real firm lesson: EVERY MUM with toddlers is just doing their absolute damn best. Especially when the odds are bloody stacked up against us with these pint-sized tornados of curiosity and chaos and seemingly inexhaustible supplies of energy. Have I mentioned that a sense of humour is IMPERATIVE in parenting? Even if I have, read it again: IMPERATIVE.

If there is ever going to be a parenting season that breaks you as a human, it's more than likely going to be when you have a toddler plus another baby at the same time. If you want to get extra crazy and really test out your capabilities as a sane person, you can have three aged under four, which is what I did.

I remember being quite perplexed when people asked me, 'And what else do you do?' after I told them I was a stay-at-home mum of three.

Sorry? I beg your pardon? Let me run you through my average day.

I wake continuously throughout the night because Bobby wants his Elsa dress, Kobe wakes at the sound of a dog barking in Queensland and Charli has cheese-rolled herself off the bed again. And keep in mind I try to be cool, calm and collected, at least until lunchtime anyway. Bobby wakes again at 4.45 a.m. because that's enough sleep for him, and decides to wake the whole house with him. Rhian 'needs to be in at work early', as he has for the last three years, so he hightails it the fuck out the door by 6.30 a.m. and I'm left to fend for myself. And then . . . there are three kids to get dressed.

'Please stand still. Don't hand me your boogers. Don't pull every single t-shirt out—okay, good, now they're all out.'

One is a diva and will try on multiple outfits; one has an aversion to clothes but, after a stand-off followed by a negotiation, will eventually headbutt himself into t-shirts and thrash about while you put shorts on him. And the baby will lie there to be dressed and wait patiently for you to pick him up so he can regurgitate whatever milk he's just had all over you, your hair and the new clothes you've just put on him. Repeat that last step about five times and finally, all kids are dressed and ready for breakfast. It is 7.00 a.m.

Charli will have toast cut into triangles with no crusts, served on a pink plate.

'Oh sorry, darling, I should have known you wanted your toast cut into alphabet letters. No, that's totally fine if you don't want to eat any of it.'

Bobby will have two bowls of cereal, two pieces of toast, a banana, a yoghurt, a muesli bar and a fruit platter, and then he'll eat some of Charli's toast too. There will be a civil war between the siblings over the toast and I'll try to referee on the sidelines, using my legs to protect Charli from Bobby's claws while also shovelling porridge into Kobe's mouth because he's started chanting foreign orders at me in 'scream'. Hair will be pulled, tears will be shed, food will be thrown.

'Please try to keep your clothes on, sweetie. Stop playing with your willy. I'd love it if you'd stop fighting. Stop feeding Kobe that. Get off him. He's not a horse.'

The place will look like there's been a colony of bin chickens on the loose and nine times out of ten Bobby will end up in his room. It is 8.00 a.m.

After cleaning what looks like a frat-house afterparty, I'll use excessive amounts of antiseptic wipes all over the kitchen and put on one of the thirteen loads of washing I'll do that day. I will then start packing a bag for the day.

'Just take your time finding your shoes. I've got all day. Oh, you want an outfit change? GOOD. Those socks are itchy? But they are the exact same brand you wore yesterday and they were fine. I can't help that your leggings crinkle, Charli. Stop pulling her hair, Bobby.'

The next three hours are crucial. If you're anything like me and have birthed a jacked-up Tasmanian devil called Bobby who lives life on fast-forward and has more energy than an eighteen-year-old raver, then you too know how important it is to drain those batteries. Kobe 'I'll never have a routine' Gerard gets thrown in the car along with everyone else, and off to a park we will go. Both boys will shit themselves on arrival.

'I told you to poo before we left home. I forgot the scooters. You never ride them anyway. Please get up off the floor, it's not the end of the world. I've got snacks.'

Charli will think she's got a UTI. It's already thirty degrees outside with ninety-nine per cent humidity, and conveniently I've broken out in a rash on 60 per cent of my body. I'll also remember that I haven't even showered and I'm actually still in my pyjama t-shirt. I will eventually find somewhere to sit down and throw snacks at them from a distance. Even though they ate an hour ago they are all ravenous, and no one starts chanting 'I'm hungry' more often than my kids do—from the second they arrive at the park.

'I'm watching. I'm watching. YES I'M WATCHING.'

'What's that on your fingers? Why is there poo on your shirt? You've been putting your fingers in your bum again. We're leaving. No, you can't have a Maccas ice cream.'

Bobby will try to steal multiple scooters from other children. Charli just wants to watch Kinder Surprise Egg unboxing videos on my phone, and I've forgotten that the third kid, whose name escapes me, is in the car. It is 11.30 a.m.

Back home for lunch. I missed a spot of porridge on the floor and now 1.5 million ants live with me. I make them lunch (the kids, not the ants), and watch as Bobby eats Charli's again. I text Rhian to tell him he needs a second and possibly a third job because I can't keep on top of their food intake, and Bobby possibly has a tapeworm.

'Give Charli her Polly Pocket back. Do not throw your supercars. You can't feed Kobe grapes.'

Hang out loads of washing, then try to sync their nap times but because Kobe only sleeps in six-minute intervals in the car, he isn't tired. Put the other two down. Kobe gets undivided attention. Play, play, sensory, boob, coochie-coochie, sleep. Have fifteen minutes of free time in which I try to reply to friends' texts from 2019, return calls and attempt to maintain a social life. Bring washing in. Hang more out. Prep dinner. It is 3.00 p.m.

Everyone wakes up. Charli wants to be carried around like a fetus, Bobby is so well-rested that he's now angry and has risen as Satan and is trying to fight me because I won't let him play inside the car on a forty-degree day, and Kobe has regurgitated his lunch all over himself, the cot, the rug and half the lounge. Strip his clothes off, put on his eighth outfit for the day, put on more washing and contemplate buying shares in Omo laundry detergent.

'One leg each. This is a four-seater lounge. If you're going to fight you can both get off me. Everyone off me. Okay, Mummy is going to lose her marbles, ha ha, no *really*. Mummy is about to blow.'

Put everyone in front of some sort of screen. Strip beds. Remake. Nosedive across the room to rescue Kobe from an affectionate body slam from Bobby. Throw my back out while Charli laughs hysterically.

'RIGHT. THAT'S IT. YOU IN THAT CORNER. YOU IN YOUR ROOM. TIME OUT.'

Walk into the backyard and scream 'FUCK!' into the air with clenched fists. Go back inside like nothing happened. It is 5.30 p.m.

Serve dinner. No one eats it. Go back outside for another 'FUCK' scream but forget I have Kobe on the boob. He now has PTSD.

'I'm sorry for yelling. Mummy didn't mean it. Could you please just stay seated at the table and at least *try* the dinner I've made for you? Who threw their dinner on the floor? Is that wee on the floor? Where is Kobe? HOLY SHIT I CAN'T TAKE ANOTHER MINUTE.'

Put everyone in the bath. Try to protect Kobe's life while also stopping his siblings from using his wiener as a shuttlecock in their invisible game of badminton. Chase kids around the house, disguising my rage with light-hearted humour and turning it into a game. *Where the fuck is Rhian?* Lord, give me strength.

Somehow dress them all for bed. Read books, sing songs and it's bedtime. It is 7.00 p.m.

Back out to the kitchen to assess the mess. How did it get so bad? Decide it would be quicker to douse the whole room in alcohol and set it on fire. Rhian arrives home. Rage at the sight of him. Pretend to feign interest in his work politics, eat dinner, scroll numbly through Instagram feed. Finally have a shower. Peek into kids' room.

Oh gosh! They are so cute when they're asleep! They smell so good. I miss them already, the little angels. I can't wait to see them in the morning.

Fall into bed and a short coma before starting the last twenty-four hours all over again. REPEAT.

Fast-forward twelve months. We had just celebrated Kobe's first birthday and now I had two toddlers and one Tibetan monk. Once Kobe was walking and all three of them were mobile, it was all over for me. I went from being a super-confident mum to a little mouse. There was one of me and three of them. I was well and truly outnumbered. They were like a small gang who took no prisoners. I didn't have enough arms to hold on to all of them or a spare knee so that all three could sit on my lap.

My appearance was the first thing that went to shit. Every now and again if I had something on I would lawnmower my legs, but I looked like I had been hit by a freight train most days. Like a deer in the headlights. *What kind of absolute fuckery is coming for me today?* I would wonder. I was dishevelled, a little frightened, covered in vomit, smelling like curdled milk and a bit of an ass, and with clothes that looked like they'd been put through a blender. I'd leave the house in my dressing gown and ugg boots during winter, and pyjama shirt and shorts in summer. Always looking defeated.

One of the most common questions—if not *the* most common question—I was asked was, 'What is it like having three small kids?' Similarly, people will ask, 'Is two kids easier than three?' and 'If you had your time over, would you have had them all so close together?' These questions usually come from people who may be sitting on the fence themselves, trying to decide whether or not to take the parenting plunge of having multiple kids close in age. It's as if they are looking to me for a glowing report, but I'm not the person who is going to tell you it's all sunshine and rainbows. Hell no. I'm going to give you cold, hard facts and help you mentally arm yourself and physically prepare for battle—oh, sorry, I mean *parenting* . . .

But sometimes people can't handle the truth. So I reply with a pros-and-cons list instead to ease them into the idea gently.

Pros

- You always have one (if not all three of them) wanting to hug you, use you as a human lounge, sleep on your chest or hold your hand. If your love language is physical touch, multiple children all at home at the same time is definitely for you.

- It's only really the first five years that you'll feel like your head has been in a blender, when your PTSD from the Mazda3 you birthed drug-free (oh wait, that was just me) is in full swing, and when you don't sleep for more than four hours a night. Five years in the grand scheme of your life isn't bad. And you'll always have botox.

- Multiple kids become a little gang that look out for each other. They become more social and when you can't be fucked getting out of your pyjamas for a day, they have built-in friends. Charli, Bobby and Kobe actually play nicely together every now and again, and are great at keeping each other entertained. They also punch on, try to scalp each other and trash each other's rooms daily, but such is sibling love.

- Hand-me-downs. After having one or two children, you won't have to buy a single thing for the rest. If they are born in different seasons, just size up and roll up the sleeves. Kobe was dressed in girls' clothes for the first two years of his life.

- You can run a tight ship like a prison officer and instead of articulating things, just shout one-word orders at them, for example: 'DINNER', 'OI', 'BATH', 'NO', 'TEETH', 'YOU', 'BED'—and they fall into line because they don't know any different.

- Because they are so close in age, they learn more from each other than they do from you. Charli basically taught Bobby how to talk, and Bobby (eventually) will be toilet-training Kobe!

- Your heart expands with each kid. You might develop a nervous twitch and become a full-time enjoyer of an alcoholic beverage, but NOTHING on earth will sound better than your child whispering 'I love you, Mum' in your ear. More kids, more love.
- It's pandemonium, in the best possible way.

Cons

- The mess is something you will NEVER be able to get on top of. Ever. Unless you plan on being in a de facto relationship with your Dyson, broom and a packet of wet wipes for the next ten years.
- Everyone is competing to be heard and for five years the noise level is constantly at 'yelling loudly'.
- Bedtime is equal parts marathon, crisis and fucken joke. Three different kids, three different ages/sets of needs, three different bedtimes—and everyone wants to be held and have lullabies sung to them. But while you are putting one to bed, another is streaking up the street after ganging up with his sister to work out the front-door deadbolt. At one point, you end up quartering a melatonin gummy to knock them the hell out and wonder how you got here.
- You're outnumbered and they know it. Whether you are partnered or doing it on your own, there are always more kids than you can carry. They strike while you are vulnerable with surprise poos and supermarket disappearing acts. It's the most terrifying in airports, Woolworths, cinemas, Westfields, non-gated playgrounds . . . pretty much anywhere outside your own home.

- You constantly have three balls in the air and have no idea which one to catch first. Your life is an exercise in determining the degrees of urgency of various life-threatening situations.
- You have to poo with two small people on your lap while the third slams the toilet seat lid into your head repeatedly.
- There are more sleep regressions than there are ants in the world.

In a short summary, it's really up to you, your level of patience and what you think you can handle. Children are the greatest gift on earth, but they don't come with a handbook and they require a lot of love and sacrifice. Your child's individual personality will also play a part because you can parent the exact same way and get three completely different children. Trust me, I know, because I have three completely different kids.

In my opinion, three has definitely been harder than two. It's like having Internet Explorer up with nineteen tabs open, eight of which are frozen, and there's a shit smell and you have no idea where the music is coming from and don't have time to investigate. But they are my world, my house feels like a home with them in it, and there is never a dull moment.

Truth be told, toddlers aren't even a roller-coaster ride. They are more like those drop-tower rides that take you all the way to the top and then plunge you instantly to the bottom. You feel like you're going to die but it's just a ride and you always survive. It's a few years of living on the edge, surrounded by unregulated emotions and unpredictability, and you really do come out the other side. Usually with a few bald spots and a nervous twitch, but otherwise unscathed.

Society will approve of us acknowledging the challenges of parenting, just as long as we refrain from expressing any potential lack of enjoyment in fulfilling that role . . . but fuck society. I have friends who love their children dearly but don't enjoy being mums. I bet so many other mums would love to admit that, but feel like they can't because they'll be judged for saying so. I know others who have chosen not to have children, and those who have regretted adding extra kids to their family—not because they don't absolutely love their children to death, but because of the strain it has put on them. You can't possibly know whether or not you are making the right decision by having kids until they are here, and then it's too late if you change your mind. Even when you think your expectations of parenting are realistic, your reality will likely be different. It's a contradictory journey that leaves you drained yet invigorated. It can suck the life out of you while simultaneously igniting your soul. It prompts endless questioning while also granting you a sense of profound understanding.

Amid the chaos of it all, there's something strangely amusing about toddlers' unpredictability. They wear their hearts on their sticky, honey-covered sleeves and remind us all that life is never dull with them around. They bring the ultimate blend of emotions and experiences: joy and sorrow, comfort and fear, love and dislike. You'll beg for bedtime to come and then you'll miss them with every part of you the minute they fall asleep. It is life's biggest paradox.

Whether we are new mums, veteran mums or something in between, I think we all experience the exact same sentiments when it comes to parenting toddlers. And we go a bit cuckoo in the process.

Just strap yourself in and enjoy the ride. It'll be over before you know it.

A LETTER TO THE DADS

Dear Rhian (and every other partner/boyfriend/husband/stepdad),

Please, please, please: when you see us playing with our kids, or even just having a cuddle with them, pick up the phone and capture the moment for us. Not because we aren't living in the moment but because the only thing better than having memories of our kids is having some kind of video or photo footage of those moments. We will never forget all the stages and the way we felt, but we will forget the details: the ringlets at the napes of their neck and how their tiny hands almost disappear in ours, the sound of their husky voices, the quirky and inexplicable things they say, their laughs, and the way they look at us like we are their everything.

I take my fair share of selfies and videos with my kids but I'm not talking about the smiling, posed ones. I'm talking about the ones when we least expect it: when we look like roadkill but we're rolling around in fits of laughter, or we're teaching a kid how to rollerskate or how to do the Nutbush.

The unfiltered real-life stuff is what I want.

Please don't make me ask.

I always pick up the phone when Rhian is playing with the kids: whether it's swimming in the pool, doing horsey rides around the house or telling an animated bedtime story.

I video as much as I can for him, because the days are long but the years are so fleeting and soon memories of them being small will be all we have. Technology means we can hold on to precious moments, and in years to come we can relive the feelings they gave us.

I could be sitting on the top of a mountain singing a Luciano Pavarotti song with my kids, as doves are released and the sunrise bathes us all in its warm glory, and it's still unlikely Rhian would stop and grab a quick ten-second video or a photo.

It's not for social media. Or for anyone else. It's for me. Do it for me. Do it for the mums. We are the love-drunk, emotionally unhinged ones who need videos to look back on at the end of the day—to help us recharge, and to remind us how far we've come and how much we gave to these little people who began life in our tummies. It would mean the world to us.

Love,

Amy

HOME

Expectation: A home similar to the one I grew up in

Reality: Manifesting works!

I think every expectation you have in life stems from your upbringing and what kind of family you were born into. Sometimes your family sets the precedent for how you want your life to go. Things you lacked as a child might be the things you would like to offer your children more of. Sometimes the way you were raised is the total opposite to how you want to raise your own children. In any case, the morals instilled in you and the perspective you have on life aren't created from thin air, but from within the four walls of your home.

I feel incredibly lucky to have been raised by the family that I was born into, and I'm very aware of the privileged upbringing that I've had. We were never wealthy, and we didn't live in a mansion on the beach or drive flashy cars. My dad used to work two jobs when my mum was raising us, but we always made ends meet, and we have always had a roof over our heads and food on the table, which I acknowledge is more than some people have. We have also been rich in things that money can't buy.

For my whole life I have wanted to replicate my own childhood and have a family unit similar to my own. As fate would have it, I went on to have exactly the same number of kids, in the same gender order too. Did I subconsciously manifest that?

After having my daughter and moving back to the area I'd grown up in, I had a newfound appreciation for my family home. Every time I popped over to visit my parents, I would find myself feeling like I was home. I'm not sure if it was the house or just the feeling I would get when I walked through the doors, but it was always so nostalgic. The bushy outlook from the backyard, which I took for granted for so many years growing up, had a calming effect on me every time I saw it. The way the wind blows through your hair and the sounds of nature (albeit loud as hell) greet you and do something good for the soul. The winter sun is always there to keep you warm, and the backyard gets almost unbearably hot in summer—and that's fine, because that's what home feels like.

I used to constantly talk to Rhian about one day being able to buy a similar house in a quiet street with wonderful neighbours. In passing, I would joke to Mum and Dad about buying the house off them when they wanted to downsize. They were both in their sixties, all three of their kids had left the nest and the house definitely didn't clean itself. But it was Dad's castle and he was more attached to it than I am to a bottle of red on a Friday night. The love he has for this home stems back three decades. It has seen some shit. It's got wounds and burn scars; it has seen heartbreaks and fights, cancer and remission, laughter and noisy Christmas parties, egg-rolling and pool parties, and, more recently, six glorious grandchildren. Truth be told, I thought they would never leave.

In 2022, my dad invited me over for a cup of tea, sat me down out the back and did the thing he does whenever he gets emotional: he puffed out his chest. He looked me in the eye and said that he and Mum wanted to move to the south coast and that they were going to put the house on the market. But, he added, if I wanted to buy it off them, I could have first dibs.

After speaking with my brothers, who didn't want to fight me for the house, Rhian and I made the best decision we've made in a long time and bought my childhood home from my parents. I'm pretty sure Dad cried himself to sleep for a few weeks because he was letting go of his castle but, as Mum pointed out, 'Better that Amy is buying it so we can come back and visit as often as we like, rather than some Joe Blow stranger', and I happen to agree with her. Nine months later, we finished renovating our home in Bangor, put it on the market, sold it in record time and moved into our new (and my old) house. We have a guest room that has Mum and Dad's name on it for whenever they want to come and stay. And the best thing is, the wonderful memories this house holds get to stay with us for another couple of decades while we make new ones in it.

The house is the place where all my expectations, hopes and dreams began, and it's brought me the one moment in which the reality matched, even exceeded, my expectations—to bring up my children in the same way (and now place) where I was brought up.

MANIFESTING WORKS, GUYS. You heard it here first. Either that, or Copp Luck just showed up unannounced again.

TURNING THIRTY-SEVEN

Expectation: Pre-pensioner era

Reality: JUST GETTING STARTED

When I was in primary school, high school kids seemed so big and mature. Then, in high school, twenty-five-year-olds seemed like grown-ups with responsibilities and credit-card debt, and thirty-seven-year-olds were basically roaming round the globe like almost-extinct dinosaurs. I remember thinking that thirty-seven was around that age you started covering your lounges with blankets and leaving the plastic permanently on your new fridge. You had a permed bob. You were middle-aged, potentially on the way to your first midlife crisis, but mostly you had your shit together and were always up-to-date with world news and politics. Your hobbies included putting coverings on your kids' schoolbooks and knitting, and you had afternoon siestas to get you through till bedtime. Teenage Amy used to think that thirty-seven was ride-public-transport-for-free old. *So old.*

But now that I am thirty-seven, I can't seem to relate to a single one of my own presumptions (although a siesta most afternoons wouldn't go astray). Not even three kids, a permanently messy house, a mortgage and 1800 bills to pay can hold me back from still feeling young at heart. The difference at thirty-seven is that I am more confident in who I am as a person than ever before. I have no inhibitions, and I know when to close doors on people and situations and when to hold them open. I really don't know shit about politics, but I know how to get everyone up on the dance floor and how to make you laugh and that's definitely something.

I know my worth, and I also know that the more kids you have, the more you drink, and that—disappointingly—at thirty-seven you just can't hold your booze or recover the same way you did in your twenties. I know I'm a demon on the dance floor and I'll forever be dancing like no one is watching, even though everyone is watching because WHO IS THAT DINOSAUR DROPPING IT LOW? And then they pull out their iPhones and film everything: *Ohhhh, look, a woman dancing and not giving a fuck. What a scene!!!* I will forever know how to have fun and I will make it a priority to fill my cup up regularly. Balance is a must at thirty-seven. My kids might make my body feel like it's ninety-eight and has just come back from competing in the Hunger Games but my soul is always alive—it just moves at a slightly slower pace and is partial to a 9 p.m. midweek bedtime.

I have truly loved my life so far. Even the hard bits. The lessons. The challenges. The heartaches and the joy. The good has always outweighed the bad and my glass-half-full approach to living in the now has never really faltered. It helps me see the potential, opportunities and silver linings in every circumstance, even the ones that hurt the most. I have loved it as a single woman, as a mother, as a wife, as a daughter and as a friend. We are all constantly evolving, and it's all for the better.

I now have three reasons to love, listen, appreciate and do better every day, and I have Rhian, the one man who knows how to hear me through the silence. My family unit is far from perfect but sometimes you only need to slow down and look at how far you've come to realise that one expectation has been met: the life you always dreamed of having is the reality of what you have right now.

Each other.

It's just like my dad always used to say: as long as we have each other, we'll always be okay.

THE REALITY OF WRITING A BOOK

Um ...

Embarking on the noble quest of writing a book is like diving headfirst into a wild labyrinth of caffeinated chaos. I pulled so many long nights that my eyes would sometimes feel like they were going to fall out of my head. Some people make writing a book their full-time job. They go away and sit on beaches, or take weekend breaks or venture to nearby libraries.

Not me. No, I just tried to fit it in around all the other things I have going on: my social media work, my podcasts, the three kids, and my myth of a husband who travels a lot for work. I remember when I first said yes to writing the book, Rhian suggested I pull back on some other work, but instead I took on more because I never listen and I thought I could juggle it all! Turns out, I could. Just not super efficiently.

Every night I would put the kids to bed and then wander downstairs in my dressing gown. First stop was always the pantry and, depending on what day of the week it was, I'd accompany my nighttime snack with either a wine or a hot chocolate. (Okay, it was mainly just wine.)

I'd sit at my kitchen table, armed with my laptop and the illusion of brilliance, ready to unleash my literary masterpiece upon the world. But I'm not a fancy writer; I'm more of a storyteller. Like I mentioned, we ain't winning any Nobel Prizes for Literature around here, but I do hope I've made you laugh.

Ideas would flow slowly like molasses as I wrote and I often found myself engaging in epic battles with my long-term friend Procrastination. Either that or I would be so exhausted from the day that most of my brain cells had already put themselves to sleep and I would just stare at a blank page. My internal voice would stage a revolt, demanding more captivating dialogue and fewer clichéd monologues about my family life. I was torn between wanting to go full steam ahead and bare it all, and being mindful that some people I talk about in the book might not want certain things discussed. But everybody mentioned in this book has read it and given me the green light, so know that I did the right thing!

In short: WRITING A BOOK IS NOT FOR THE FAINT-HEARTED.

But it's been real. And super stressful. And loads of fun. And above all, I'm proud of me. I really wanted to do the book justice and I want you to be reading it in my tone of voice. I'm a little bit rough around the edges—in a good way—and so is this book, I think.

It's a huge accomplishment for me. BRB . . . just changing my title to AUTHOR . . .

My final parting words to anyone reading this book:

Find the good light in your life.

ZOOM IN.
And focus.
Love you all.
The end. xx

ACKNOWLEDGEMENTS

HA this is wild, I can't believe I am writing an 'ACKNOW-LEDGEMENTS' section in my very own book. I wish you could see the look on my face right now. I'm sitting at my kitchen table with a large, slightly creepy grin on my face just staring at my laptop. I'm also not wearing pants which makes this weirder.

I have no idea if there is a right or wrong way to write an acknowledgements chapter but here goes.

I'd just like to thank the Academy . . .

Okay, just kidding.

I want to thank Tessa from Allen and Unwin. She has not only been the most wonderful human on earth in terms of putting up with my scatteredness but she has also doubled as a counsellor. She's let me unpack some random life truths/stories that she has absolutely no idea about and she's just held space for me, listened and offered advice. She's helped me word difficult chapters better and steered my neck in the right direction and propelled me forward. She has checked in on me monthly and given me feedback constantly along the way! She's also given me deadlines which is the exact type of ass-whooping I need and above all she has believed in me, which has been paramount for this book's success. Can't thank you enough Tess. X

And secondly, I want to thank my family. Rhian in particular. As a mum I've been operating at about seventy per cent but as a wife, it's been more like thirty per cent. Our only one-on-one time together is normally when the kids go down to bed at night, but the last six months I have left him on the couch alone so I could write this book. He has never complained once. (Okay, maybe there were one or two complaints along the way, but he has otherwise shown me unconditional support.) He's picked up the slack with the kids and helped me by getting them ready in the mornings and making lunch boxes for school before he goes to work because I've only come to bed at 2 a.m. It's been a bit of a juggle and from a health perspective I wouldn't say it's advisable but I finished this book and I wouldn't have been able to do it without him. Every week he tells me how proud of me he is. It's hard to put into words the feeling he gives me. It's an invisible pump-up that allows me to keep going, even when I'm so tired I feel like slipping into a coma. So so grateful we chose each other. I will love him until the day I die.

And to my kids, Charli, Bobby and Kobe—sorry Mum has been a bit of an unhinged psychopath the last couple of months, I know I haven't been able to lay next to you in bed for as long as you normally like and I've been a bit of a walking zombie some mornings, but one day when you read this book (not for at least a decade) I hope that it makes you proud. I hope it makes you realise that life will constantly ebb and flow but perspective and gratitude are everything and that I will always be your number-one supporter in life and help you to achieve anything you want to, just like your dad did for me with this book. Love you more than all the stars in the sky.

ACKNOWLEDGEMENTS

And to Big B and the Mustang—thank you for being my number-one role models and for setting the most wonderful benchmark when it comes to living life. So many chapters and expectations in this book are because you paved the way for me and gave me something to strive for. Sorry there's a few swear words in here. Above all I hope I've made you proud and I hope you know how much love and respect I have for you.